JB JOSSEY-BASS

UP THE
ORGANIZATION*

*How to Stop the Corporation
from Stifling People and
Strangling Profits

Commemorative Edition

Robert Townsend

Foreword by Warren Bennis

John Wiley & Sons, Inc.

Published by Jossey-Bass
A Wiley Imprint
989 Market Street, San Francisco, CA 94103-1741   www.josseybass.com

Wiley Bicentennial logo: Richard J. Pacifico

Jossey-Bass books and products are available through most bookstores. To contact Jossey-Bass directly call our Customer Care Department within the U.S. at 800-956-7739, outside the U.S. at 317-572-3986, or fax 317-572-4002.

Jossey-Bass also publishes its books in a variety of electronic formats. Some content that appears in print may not be available in electronic books.

The chapter titled "Further 'Up the Organization'" was originally published in the July 1970 issue of *Playboy*.

Library of Congress Cataloging-in-Publication Data

Townsend, Robert, 1920-1998
        Up the organization : how to stop the corporation from stifling people and strangling profits / Robert Townsend ; foreword by Warren Bennis. — Commemorative ed.
        p. cm.
        ISBN 978-0-7879-8775-6 (cloth)
        1. Management. I. Title.
HD31.T67 2007
        658—dc22   2007007195

Printed in the United States of America
FIRST EDITION
HB Printing   10 9 8 7 6 5 4 3 2 1

Warren Bennis (signature)

A WARREN BENNIS BOOK

This collection of books is devoted exclusively to new and exemplary contributions to management thought and practice. The books in this series are addressed to thoughtful leaders, executives, and managers of all organizations who are struggling with and committed to responsible change. My hope and goal is to spark new intellectual capital by sharing ideas positioned at an angle to conventional thought—in short, to publish books that disturb the present in the service of a better future.

BOOKS IN THE WARREN BENNIS SIGNATURE SERIES

CONTENTS

"Where Have You Gone, Joe DiMaggio?"

It was sometime in 1967 when I was teaching at MIT, and my office phone rang. It was Bob Townsend. Not his secretary, mind you, but the real Bob Townsend. He was already known as something of a CEO icon(oclast), having revived a moribund car rental business, Avis, with the audacity of a kid with a spray can looking for trouble. He'd already taken his famous jab at the #1 Hertz with the killer commercial, "WE'RE ONLY #2, BUT WE TRY HARDER." He had just resigned and wondered if he should write a book based on his Avis experience. He didn't read business books, he told me; he thought they were written by monastic types who had never experienced the smoky complexity of real work, who might not even know how to start a car, let alone lead people. The only exception, he told me, was my late mentor, Doug McGregor, who had written an extraordinarily influential book, *The Human Side of Enterprise*, which shaped the foundation of the field nowadays referred to as organizational behavior ("OB"). He had also heard that Doug insisted that all of his Ph.D. students work every summer for a blue-collar manufacturing company. (I spent two summers at

Dewey & Almy, a pesticide company in nearby Lexington.)
That's why Bob Townsend was calling me—to learn more
about McGregor and his ideas.

Bob asked if he could come to Boston sometime to talk.
When do you have time? I said, "Now." He knocked on the
front door of my house that same afternoon, a Friday, and stayed
the weekend. He was captivated by McGregor's famous cate-
gorization of human nature, for which he coined the terms
Theory Y and Theory X. Perhaps overly simple? Bob didn't
think so, nor did I. The two philosophies of leadership, almost
Manichaean in their dichotomous assumptions and metaphysics,
are still evident today, despite Doug's encouraging optimism:

> The ancient conception that people do the work of
> the world only if they are forced to do so by threats
> or intimidation, or by the camouflaged authoritarian
> methods of paternalism, has been suffering from a
> lingering fatal illness for a quarter of a century. I ven-
> ture to guess that it will be dead in another decade.
> (*The Professional Manager,* edited by W. Bennis and
> C. McGregor, McGraw-Hill, 1968)

In this book, Townsend translates Theory X based on
three (dubious) propositions:

- *People hate to work.*
- *They have to be driven and threatened with punishment to
  get them to toward organizational objectives.*
- *They like security, aren't ambitious, want to be told what to
  do, dislike responsibility.*

Townsend's rendition of Theory Y is based on three quite
different propositions:

- *People don't hate work. It's as natural as rest or play.*
- *They don't have to be forced or threatened. If they commit themselves to mutual objectives, they'll drive themselves more effectively than you can drive them.*
- *But they'll commit themselves only to the extent they can see ways of satisfying their ego and development needs.*

Before I wrote this Foreword, I played a little game. I put the book in the palm of my right hand and stroked the edge of pages from back to front. I then stopped at random and wrote down the lead or other sentences that caught my eye. Here are a few examples:

- page xxvi: *Big successful institutions aren't successful because of the way they operate, but in spite of it. They didn't get to the top doing things the way they're doing them now.*
- page 10: *Call yourself up. When you're off on a business trip or a vacation, pretend you're a customer. Telephone some part of your organization and ask for help. You'll run into some real horror shows. Then trying calling yourself up and see what indignities you've built into your own defenses.*
- page 54: *Billy Graham has a man named Grady Wilson who yells "Horseshit"—however you say that in Baptist— at him whenever he takes himself too seriously. Perhaps that is one of the reasons the Graham organization has been so successful. Every chief executive should find someone to perform this function and then make sure he can be fired only for being too polite.*
- page 63: *True leadership must be for the benefit of the followers, not the enrichment of the leaders.*
- page 104: *The world is divided into two classes of people: the few people who make good on their promises (even if they don't promise as much), and the many who don't. Get in column A and stay there. You'll be very valuable wherever you are.*

- page 115: *Secrecy: A child's garden of diseases.*
- page 151: *The best acquisitions will look overpriced and you'll be tempted to veto them on that score. Don't—not if everything else looks right. The bag of snakes will come disguised as an ever-loving blue-eyed bargain.*

I used to think of Bob Townsend as *the* management guru of the Sixties. With just a little imagination, the irreverent title of this book could double as a hippie curse: *UP **YOUR** ORGANIZATION.* Thinking about Bob and his work and life, Ken Kesey's magnificent touchstone of the Sixties, *One Flew Over the Cuckoo's Nest* came to mind. Nurse Ratchet was the very model of The Bureaucrat: unfeeling, dispassionate, analytical, concerned only with the smooth functioning of the asylum. Her nemesis, McMurtry, was played unforgettably by the irrepressible rebel, Jack Nicholson. "Up yours," he was saying, without lifting a finger.

Bob's prose also brings to mind that other totem of the period, the movie, *The Graduate.* Will anybody of a certain age forget that scene when Braddock (Dustin Hoffman) was given unwanted advice by a prosperous and pompous businessman, both of them standing, belly deep, in an upscale Beverly Hills swimming pool:

Braddock: "Yes, sir."
Businessman: "Are you listening?"
Braddock: "Yes. I am."
Businessman: "**Plastics!**"

Despite appearances, Bob Townsend is not just a Sixties happening. His words still ring true, truer than they seemed almost forty years ago. Like McGregor, he may have been stricken with a case of unwarranted optimism. Doug thought we'd have an anti–Theory X vaccine by 1980. It is undeniable that Theory Y has gained more adherents and robustness over the years with a new vocabulary of "HR talk" like empowerment, transparency, agency, and so forth. And there are certainly more enlightened and emboldened leaders and scholars making some headway toward creating cultures of growth and learning. But it will always be a struggle. And we need, *seriously* need, more Bob Townsends. More leaders and scholars who make us nervous with their ideas, who bother us, bother the hell out of us. Ray Bradbury put it nicely in *Fahrenheit 451*:

> We need not to be let alone. We need to be really bothered once in awhile. How long has it been since you were really bothered? About something important, about something real?

Bob Townsend was one helluva botherer, always reminding us of what's important. Unlike those other ephemeral botherers of the Sixties, his songs live on and on, just like that Simon & Garfunkel favorite, "Mrs. Robinson":

> Where have you gone Joe DiMaggio, a nation turns its lonely eyes to you . . .

January 2007   Warren Bennis

PUBLISHER'S NOTE

The core text of this commemorative edition of *Up the Organization* is drawn from the reprint edition that was published in 1971 by Fawcett. The A-to-Z portion of the reprint was almost identical to that of the 1970 Knopf hardcover. (Townsend added to the paperback a small number of annotations and a preface titled "What This Book Is.") The two appendixes "Further 'Up the Organization'" and "Guerrilla Guide for Working Women" were written just after the hardcover appeared and were added to the Fawcett paperback. Although nearly all of Townsend's observations are timeless in their perspicacity, his advice to the working women of 1970 does not seem as germane today. (There had yet to be a female CEO of a Fortune 500 company at the time of his writing.) For this reason, the publishers of this edition decided to drop the "Guerrilla Guide."

Further Up the Organization appeared in 1984 and was a significantly different book. With only two exceptions, however, Townsend never withdrew anything he said in the original edition; he merely tried to update or add variations to his theme. (These exceptions are noted in the text.) He *was* particularly diligent to remove references that will sound sexist to the current-day reader. The publisher has made note of this where appropriate so that the reader may not judge Townsend unfairly. It is worth noting that many of the "new" chapters in the 1984 edition began their life as part of his "Further 'Up the Organization'" appendix.

Townsend added his own annotations in the first edition using an asterisk. These have been carried over exactly as they appeared in the original. Notes from the publisher or editor in this edition are intended for general reference and are labeled "Editor's Note."

Robert Townsend's Cure for Management Heartburn

James O'Toole, research professor, University of Southern California; author of fifteen books, including *Leadership A to Z,* a tribute to the life and work of Robert Townsend.

It is often said that Peter Drucker invented management; if so, Robert Townsend invented leadership. It was Townsend who, in the 1960s, first made Avis "Try Harder" and then wrote the 1970 best seller *Up the Organization* to help other CEOs stop their own corporations "from stifling people and strangling profits." His gutsy stance—in both practice and theory—would radically change the roles of those who subsequently occupied the executive suites of large corporations.

Prior to Townsend's transformation of Avis, Fortune 500 companies had been headed, variously, by entrepreneurs, inventors, financial geniuses, managers, bureaucrats, men in gray flannel suits, crown princes, dictators, petty satraps, and unimaginative combinations of the above. But Townsend was the first true, modern corporate leader (*def:* one who manifests vision, integrity, and courage in a consistent pattern of behavior that inspires trust, motivation, and responsibility on the part of followers, who in turn become leaders themselves).

Townsend's disciples have led many companies, including at least three remarkable start-ups with which I'm personally familiar: Gordon Forward, CEO of Chapparal Steel, introduced a Townsendian "management by adultery" (a previously X-rated concept in which Forward treated his employees like adults and then got out of the way as they set productivity records); Bob Davids, CEO of Radica Games, predicated his leadership philosophy on two simple Townsend commandments ("Don't con anybody—including yourself," and "Treat people with respect") and went on to create a $230 million company from scratch by becoming a toy-industry leader in technical design; and Jacques Raiman, CEO of the GSI Corporation in the 1980s, led France into the computer age with a breakthrough philosophy of bureaucracy bashing and employee involvement. When asked where he had learned to lead in such a non-Gallic way, Raiman shocked French friends by reaching into his pocket and pulling out a dog-eared paperback edition of *Up the Organization* (in English, no less). Quel horreur!

Townsend became a role model for many leaders because they responded to his candor, spontaneity, and integrity. When they met Bob, they understood why it makes sense to treat people the way you would want to be treated if you were in their shoes. He never engaged in Machiavellian machination or manipulation (he treated everyone as an end, never as a means), and he was free of the hubris that afflicts too many CEOs. Townsend always said "we" and never engaged in the pathetic craving for credit, adulation, and center stage that often characterizes executive behavior.

Townsend was probably the funniest CEO who ever made big bucks in big business. (Admittedly, CEOs aren't bred to maximize the wit gene—but he was funny even compared with those in such clownish fields as law, politics, and journalism.) Because he directed barbed advice at the powerful, he sometimes was not well received on the Chautauqua circuit, where the rule of thumb was the Eleventh Commandment: never speak ill of those who pay the bill. Townsend refused to kiss up: "Directors are usually the friends of the chief executive put there to keep him safely in office," he said, sticking a finger in the eye of the indolently powerful. Thus, "be sure to serve cocktails and a heavy lunch before the [board] meeting. At least one of the older directors will fall asleep (literally) at the meeting and the consequent embarrassment will make everyone eager to get the whole mess over as soon as possible."

Humor aside, Townsend was appalled by the yes-men and (later) yes-women who dominated U.S. boardrooms, and he was one of the first to promote shareholder advocacy among outside directors. Anticipating Jack Welch, Townsend had disdain for CEOs who sat on other boards: "No outside directorships and trusteeships for the chief executive. . . . You can't even run your own company, dummy." And he castigated dilettantish professional directors who sit on twelve boards and contribute to none. Heresy!

Further, Townsend was the first corporate chief to practice what is just now being preached in the best-led corporations: no reserved parking spaces, no org. charts, no job descriptions, no short-term pandering to Wall Street, no company planes, no golf club memberships. On the positive side: stock options (not backdated!) for *everybody*, honesty as the best policy, reinvestment for the long haul, rewards for performance, commitment to product (service) quality, true delegation, encouragement of healthy dissent, and, above all, the virtue of putting customers first. You heard it right: he practiced all the above in the 1960s.

Townsend hated bureaucracy and bloated central headquarters. His advice: "Fire the P.R. Department." Ditto the law, purchasing, and other staffs headed by "V.P.'s of." "Fire the Personnel Department," he said most famously, not only because those supernumeraries produce little at great expense but, more important, because no significant contribution to corporate excellence had ever been led by an H.R. department. So why not get rid of it? Sacrilege!

OK, so Townsend was a bit controversial. But that's a characteristic of great leadership, and Bob didn't back down when critics turned up the heat. He didn't care what people thought about him personally; what he cared about was creating an organization that was both profitable and an exciting place to work. In short, Bob changed people's lives by involving and energizing them in the process of creating a better future for their organizations. Bob changed lives by giving people the courage of their convictions.

In March 1970, fresh out of grad school and working at my first real job, I found myself suffering from chronic management heartburn. Searching for a cure, I had tried everything—deep breathing, Tums, reciting Bible verses—but nothing worked. Then, on one extended lunchtime foray, by chance I picked up a hot-off-the-press copy of Townsend's book. I took three quick doses and felt better immediately.

Emboldened, I went to my boss and told him how we too could become an innovative, productive organization where people would actually enjoy coming to work. In measured tones, he explained that this would occur only over my dead body (my body, mind you, not his). I took the hint, cleared off my desk, descended forty-eight floors to street level, and never went back. Ever since, whenever I've felt a case of organizational blues coming on, I've dug into *Up the Organization* for a booster shot of uncommon common sense.

How Robert Townsend Talked Me out of Getting an MBA

Bob Davids, cofounder and former CEO, Radica Games; owner, Sea Smoke Cellars

I honestly tell people that I tried to build the culture of our company around *Up the Organization* and Robert Townsend's ideas. Before we even began to build Radica, Townsend had already taught me that you cannot "manage" people. I still cringe when somebody describes "managing" another human being. Although he was one of the most inspiring leaders I've met, Bob was also adamant that leaders can't motivate anyone—they can only create the environment where individuals motivate themselves. In my own imperfect way, I tried to put Bob's lessons into practice at Radica—he deserves as much of the credit for Radica's success as I do, and neither of us deserve as much credit as the nearly eight thousand employees who built the company.

I first met Townsend in 1981 when he joined the board of International Game Technology (IGT), where I was director of engineering and industrial design. There was a knock on my office door, and Bob asked if he could have fifteen minutes of my time—he left five hours later. In those five hours, Bob asked me about my ambitions and passions, and discussed my career plans. When I told him I planned to pursue an executive MBA, he strongly discouraged this and told me that what I'd really need is an education in leadership—he said the world had plenty of managers but far too few true leaders. I had never heard of *Up the Organization,* but I was strongly moved by our talk. I stopped at the bookstore on the way home from work and read it that night. As it turned out, I later followed Bob's advice and attended the leadership program at Cal Tech.

As great minds and leaders often do, Bob Townsend articulated ideas that most of us know intuitively but don't know how to express consciously. I had had some leadership roles going back to the surfboard shop I managed, but I had never had a framework for leading other than the traditional model. I knew I didn't want to boss people around, and Townsend finally gave me the language for what I'd call egalitarian leadership. In essence, I learned that I needed to subordinate myself to those I led. Your job as leader is get to the lowest level and find out the tools your people need—whether it's a shovel or a computer—to get the job done. When we were starting up shop in China, the employees were shocked when I got down into a ditch with them to help build a drain. The most important currency of leadership is time. If you commit your time to your people and create an atmosphere and a perception of fairness, you will earn their respect, and your organization will achieve results far beyond anyone's expectations. Encouragement is important, but any attempt at external motivation is negative. If you don't screw up, your employees will motivate themselves—that's their job.

Bob's ideas were so important to me, I was determined to get him on the board when Radica went public in 1994. We had never run into each other again after our 1981 meeting, and not surprisingly, Bob had completely forgotten about me and our conversation. He rebuffed me politely when I

approached him through a mutual contact. I asked my friend
to try him again and tell him that I "rejected his rejection."
No go. I still don't know how I convinced my friend to give
Townsend a third try, and told him that he couldn't reject
Radica until he knew our story. I only wanted one hour of his
time, and Townsend agreed to meet at the Biltmore Hotel
with his friend Jim O'Toole. Several hours later, both Jim and
Bob were on the board. I once inadvertently heard Bob tell a
new board member that he had had more fun on the board
of our "little company" than on any other; that was one of my
proudest moments.

Bob was an invaluable asset on the board; although he
was not chairman, he was the natural soul of the group and
set the tone. He forbade anyone to mention the "S word"—
stock price. He was smooth and confident in everything and
helped mediate some difficult board and personality issues as
if they were mere speed bumps. He asked me once a month
to put everything that was wrong at Radica on one sheet of
paper—he'd told me he'd assume the best if I didn't tell him
otherwise. If a memo about a problem ever exceeded one page,
he told me I didn't understand the problem. Once a year, he
asked for a one-page plan in case I went down in an airplane—
that was the beginning of our succession planning. When he
joined the board, I followed his example in the book and
wrote out my resignation letter, which I presented to him
yearly. The irony is that he wouldn't accept my resignation
when I really meant it. I was finally able to remind him that
he wrote that no CEO should stay in the job for more than
five years—I lasted seven.

Having spent so much time using and discussing the
book, I discovered two important things putting it into practice. First, and most important, I found that Townsend's ideas
cross borders perfectly well, even into a culture that many claim
is strongly "top-down" and patriarchal. Ninety-four percent of

Radica's employees were in China, and I spent six years on the ground there leading the company's growth. Some who felt they understood Chinese culture argued that I shouldn't weaken my status by engaging in menial tasks at times or spending so much time on the factory floor. When I moved to China, I found the oldest, rattiest desk and moved it into the middle of the office floor with seventy people—I didn't have a corner office. I flew coach and didn't have a fancy company car. The employees could see, hear, and touch what I was trying to do. They could listen to the deals and conversations I made on the phone. The results and growth we achieved speak for themselves—we became the third most profitable toy company in the world in three years. Once our employees could see I was dedicated to fairness and to supporting them, I had gained their respect and allegiance.

The time came when I would have to call on that respect. And when I faced a cash crisis, even our board wanted me to get off the factory floor to solve it. But Bob backed me up and understood that I wasn't going to solve the crisis—our people were. I told our team the trouble we were facing and explained the numbers. I asked them what we needed to do, and they came up with a plan to cut expenses by 60 percent. It wasn't *my* plan; it was *their* plan. They didn't know that the CFO and the board had told me we needed to make cuts of 63 percent. If I had gone into that room and forced those cuts, there would have been a fight. But I was honest about the problems, and they motivated themselves to solve them; I couldn't do that for them.

I should add that we weathered that storm and returned to profitability, and we didn't do that by gutting our innovation efforts. In the long run, we had to innovate our way out of the problem—and our people did come up with some breakout products that dominated the market. When Radica finally merged with Mattel in 2006 after I left the company, it was valued at $224 million.

The second important point I've taken away from using *Up the Organization* these many years is that it's almost impossible for an already large company to adopt the book's ideas. This may sound harsh, and it goes against some of the spirit of the book, but I feel that it's true. Bob's ideas *can* work if they're hard-wired into the culture of the company at startup. If you wait too long, institutionalization, inertia, and politics will defeat guerrilla leadership. Bob as much as admitted this to me when I asked him directly for examples of large companies that were able to make the switch from Theory X to Theory Y. He rattled off a half dozen examples, including IBM, where the effort had ultimately failed. The other successful example he cited to me was Chaparral Steel in Texas, which was roughly the same size as Radica. I consider Southwest Airlines during the Kelleher years to be a prime example of egalitarian leadership in a company. The large airlines tried to imitate Southwest's culture in some ways, but they never grasped the secret of Southwest's success. The CEO of American Airlines never made it a practice to stand at the ticket counter and check bags. Herb Kelleher wasn't afraid to lead from the bottom up—and he created that culture from the start.

More than anything else, I want anyone reading this to know that I touched greatness when I crossed paths with Robert Townsend. The little bit that rubbed off on me and the culture of Radica—and now Sea Smoke Cellars—is the source of any success I have had.

Up the Publisher: On Editing Robert Townsend

Robert Gottlieb, formerly editor in chief, Alfred A. Knopf

Robert Townsend was a true original. From the beginning of our work together as editor and author, he entirely lived up to the spirit of his book. He didn't have a literary agent, and he refused to negotiate his publishing contract. In our first conversation, he made three things clear to me:

1. He didn't want to waste any time worrying about financial and business details of the book's publication. We could spend as much time as we wanted to discuss the editorial content of the book; he'd just trust that we knew our jobs as publishers.
2. In recognition of the trust he placed in us, he asked only that we give him the best financial arrangement that worked with our numbers. He didn't want to talk about this; he just wanted me to know that he expected us to be fair.
3. Finally, he wouldn't read the contract we sent him—he'd just go to the final page and sign it. He wouldn't show the contract to any lawyers; if he did so, we'd talk about the contract for years, and the book would never be published.

Needless to say, we went out of our minds making sure that he got the best possible publishing agreement.

Because his office was in New York, Bob visited us frequently—often unannounced. He seemed to enjoy our meetings, and we were always glad to see him. Let's just say our conversations could be freewheeling. A chance observer might have concluded that he was, well, a nutcase, and in truth, his energy and enthusiasm could be wearing at times. But from the creative point of view, he was absolutely brilliant. For example, we at Knopf never really liked his title, *Up the Organization*. It just seemed too odd, and we were always trying to come up with something better. Bob would gladly have tossed it for a superior alternative, but we never found one. We ended up making the best of what he had given us. Needless to say, Bob's title turned out to be a stroke of genius, which just goes to show how much publishers know about their business.

The book was so good and so unique that I assumed it would be "big," but I never expected it to be the explosive best seller it turned out to be. We had our first sign of what was to come just after the prepublication excerpt appeared in *Harper's*. On the first day the magazine hit the stands, a half dozen desperate people appeared at the Knopf reception desk looking for the book. I haven't seen that happen before or since. At that time, a book that sold 100,000 copies in hardcover was a great success. *Up the Organization* broke 300,000 copies in just a few months. It was certainly one of the most successful books I've edited.

I believe the secret of the book's success was that everything Bob said and advised exactly reflected the way he behaved. His ideas were original, and they worked. His book is so provocative that it would be easy to label him a provocateur. In my view, however, he was a secular prophet—somebody who fervently preached exactly as he practiced. There was no room for hypocrisy in his writing or his life. Business fads may come and go, but there will always be a need for such pure voices in the wilderness.

TO DONALD PETRIE

"And God created the Organization and gave It dominion over man."

Genesis 1, 30A, Subparagraph VIII

WHAT THIS BOOK IS

Up the Organization is a survival manual for successful corporate guerrillas. It is a book about how institutions—groups of people working together for a common purpose—*ought* to conduct themselves. If you get a chance to use it, please consider two things carefully:

1. Big successful institutions aren't successful *because* of the way they operate, but in spite of it. They didn't get to the top doing things the way they're doing them now.
2. I really mean every word I say in this book. I've tested it all in practice. It works. But if it's going to work for you, you have to adapt it to *your* personality. Don't be timid. Give it your own style, timing, and follow-through, or throw it away.

The main point: to get you and the people you work with fired-up to achieve whatever goals you select.

And always remember: getting there isn't half the fun—it's all the fun.

MEMORANDUM

To: *The Reader*
From: *The Author*
Subject: *How to Use* Up the Organization

This book is in alphabetical order. Using the table of contents, which doubles as the index, you can locate any subject on the list in thirteen seconds. And you can read all I have to say about it in five minutes or less.

Dip into it someplace.★ If you don't get at least a hollow laugh *and* a sharpened need to kick that 200-foot sponge you work for, then throw the book away. It's not for you. There are already too many organizational orthodoxies imposed on people, and I don't want to help the walking dead institute another one.

In the average company the boys in the mailroom, the president, the vice-presidents, and the girls in the steno pool have three things in common: they are docile, they are bored, and they are dull. Trapped in the pigeonholes of organization charts, they've been made slaves to the rules of private and public hierarchies that run mindlessly on and on because nobody can change them.

So we've become a nation of office boys. Monster corporations like General Motors and monster agencies like the Defense Department have grown like cancer until they take up nearly all of the living working-space. Like clergymen in Anthony Trollope's day, we're but mortals trained to serve immortal institutions.

★ On second thought, read "People" first—it's the place to start.

This is not our natural state. Most of us come from good solid European stock whose record of rapacity, greed, cruelty, and treachery would make Genghis Khan look like Mahatma Gandhi. To go down now without a whimper (much less a bang) is completely out of character.

Two solutions confront each of us:

Solution One *is the cop-out: you can decide that what is must be inevitable; grab your share of the cash and fringes; and comfort yourself with the distractions you call leisure.*

Solution Two *is nonviolent guerrilla warfare: start dismantling our organizations where we're serving them, leaving only the parts where they're serving us. It will take millions of such subversives to make much difference.*

This book is about Solution Two.

It's for those who have the courage, the humor, and the energy to make a non-monster company, or a non-monster piece of a monster company, operate as if people were human.

All you need is a talent for spotting the idiocies now built into the system. But you'll have to give up being an administrator who loves to run others and become a manager who carries water for his people so they can get on with the job. And you'll have to keep a suspicious eye on the phonies who cater to your uncertainties or feed your trembling ego on press releases, office perquisites, and optimistic financial reports. You'll have to give substance to such tired rituals as the office party. And you'll certainly have to recognize, once you get a hunk of your company's stock, that you aren't the last man who might enjoy the benefits of shareholding. These elegant simplicities require a sense of justice that won't be easy to hang on to.

I wrote this book when I realized how friends in one small company were being diverted by the glitter of the monster models: *if Time Inc. puts its executives in fancy offices, that must be the way to be big.* Model-watching has both a crude and subtle influence upon people at every level in every kind of work. To help start a countermovement in that company, I Xeroxed a draft of this book and left a copy on each desk before anybody got to work.

If you master each section and focus your imagination on helping your employees get everything they can deserve, you and they will probably come back to life and get rich.

Don't blame me if that doesn't solve any of your problems.

Editor's Note: Brian Sellstrom, former CFO of CRM, Inc., of Del Mar, California, confirms Townsend's account and CRM's identity as "the small company" mentioned here. Sellstrom still has a copy of the memo that was left on his chair and reports that it was titled "ABC Survival Manual." CRM was the parent company of Psychology Today *before it was sold to Ziff-Davis; its textbook division was sold to Random House, and its films division was later sold to McGraw-Hill. The original company lives on today as CRM Learning, in Carlsbad, California, where it is a respected provider of business training programs.*

CONTENTS

A ADVERTISING

Fire the whole advertising department and your old agency. Then go get the best new agency you can. And concentrate your efforts on making it fun for them to create candid, effective advertising for you. Unless you've just done this, the odds favor that you have a bunch of bright people working at cross purposes to produce—at best—mediocre ads. We started at Avis by asking a few people for a list of the hottest agencies. Then we called on the creative heads of those agencies and tried to interest them in the rent a car business. Ultimately we stumbled on the right question: "How do we get five million dollars of advertising for one million dollars?" (our competition has five dollars for each dollar we have, and yet we have to pay the same price for cars, insurance, rent, gas, oil, and people).

Finally, Bill Bernbach heard the question and answered: "If you want five times the impact, give us ninety days to learn enough about your business to apply our skills, and then run every ad we write where we tell you to run it. Our people work to see how effective their ideas are. But most clients put our ads through a succession of Assistant V.P.'s and V.P.'s of advertising, marketing, and legal until we hardly recognize the remnants. If you promise to run them just as we write them, you'll have every art director and copywriter in my shop moonlighting on your account."

We shook hands on it.★

★ To keep people at Avis and at Doyle Dane Bernbach from violating Bernbach's vision of the ideal account, I wrote "The Avis Rent A Car Advertising Philosophy," had it framed, and hung it in everyone's office (at both client and agency). It reads:

Ninety days later, Bill Bernbach came out to show Avis his recommended ads. He said he was sorry but the only honest things they could say were that the company was second largest and that the people were trying harder. Bernbach said his own research department had advised against the ads, that he didn't like them very much himself—but it was all they had so he was recommending them. We didn't like them much at Avis either, but we had agreed to run whatever Bill recommended.

The rest is history. Our internal sales growth rate increased from 10 per cent to 35 per cent in the next couple of years.

Moral: **Don't hire a master to paint you a masterpiece and then assign a roomful of schoolboy-artists to look over his shoulder and suggest improvements.**

Avis Rent A Car
Advertising Philosophy

1. Avis will never know as much about advertising as DDB, and DDB will never know as much about the rent a car business as Avis.

2. The purpose of the advertising is to persuade the frequent business renter (whether on a business trip, a vacation trip, or renting an extra car at home) to try Avis.

3. A serious attempt will be made to create advertising with five times the effectiveness (see #2 above) of the competition's advertising.

4. To this end, Avis will approve or disapprove, not try to improve, ads which are submitted. Any changes suggested by Avis must be grounded on a material operating defect (a wrong uniform for example).

5. To this end, DDB will only submit for approval those ads which they as an agency recommend. They will not "see what Avis thinks of that one."

6. Media selection should be the primary responsibility of DDB. However, DDB is expected to take the initiative to get guidance from Avis in weighting of markets or special situations, particularly in those areas where cold numbers do not indicate the real picture. Media judgments are open to discussion. The conviction should prevail. Compromises should be avoided.

ALPHABETICAL ORDER

Make sure that whoever types your infrequent memos (*see* Memorandum, the Last) uses alphabetical order. Otherwise some of your people will go through Freudian agonies as their names rise and fall on the addressee list and they appear to rise and fall in your favor.

ASSISTANTS-TO AND MAKE-WORKING

The only people who thoroughly enjoy being assistants-to are vampires. The assistant-to operates in a very different way from an assistant. The regular line assistant has the authority of his boss when his boss is away and can therefore make the tactical day-to-day decisions that permit the surrounding areas of the company to keep functioning.

The differences can be seen by drawing three kinds of organizations:

1. Best organization.

2. Twenty-five per cent less effective. Each level of management lowers communication effectiveness within the organization by about 25 per cent.

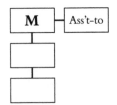

3. The absolute worst. Usually the sign of a weak, ineffective manager.

The assistant-to recommends itself to the weak or lazy manager as a crutch. It helps him where he shouldn't and can't be helped—head-to-head contact with his people. A good man deserves direct confrontation with his boss—especially when they're not in full accord. If all he gets is visits and memos from an assistant-to, he's entitled to blow his stack and go find a smarter boss somewhere.

There are some intelligent people doing assistant-to work: getting between the boss and the people who report to him, usurping power, crossing wires, and draining the organization's strength and zeal. You can't really blame the assistant-to. He wound up there because the boss got overworked and then followed his instincts. Instead of giving pieces of his job to other line officers, or carving out a whole job and giving it to someone to run with, he hired an assistant-to, and immediately became much less effective than he was when he was just overworked.

Another problem. You can't tell an assistant-to by his title. Some are called V.P. or Senior V.P. or Executive V.P. or even Chairman of the Executive Committee. But you can always tell one by the way he operates. He moves back and forth between the boss and his people with oral or written messages on real or apparent problems—overlapping and duplicating efforts and make-working.

In my book anyone who has an assistant-to should be fined a hundred dollars a day until he eliminates the position.

B BIBLIOGRAPHY

By far the best two books I've ever read on the subject of getting things done through organizations are: *Managing for Results* by Peter F. Drucker, New York, Harper & Row, 1964, and *The Human Side of Enterprise* by Douglas McGregor, New York, McGraw-Hill, 1960.

Editor's Note: Both books remain in print after forty years. Managing for Results *is available in paperback from Collins;* The Human Side of Enterprise *is still published by McGraw-Hill.*

BIG WHEELS IN LITTLE COMPANIES

Small companies can hire big-company retirees when the man is going to exercise specific skills. It doesn't matter how big or little the company is. But it won't work with generalists. Small companies must be Spartan to survive. Big companies are small companies that succeeded. Most of them have become epicurean institutions. And their fat cats have developed a lot of bad habits.

I know one small outfit that hired a big-company generalist as president when he retired. His first four acts were:

1. *Put his son-in-law on the payroll as his assistant-to.*
2. *Order a private bathroom built next to his office.*
3. *Order a reserved parking space in front of the building.*
4. *Take his wife on a three-month trip around the world.*

It almost killed the little company.

BOSS, HOW TO RETIRE THE

The most successful retirement I ever saw was that of Walter L. Jacobs, founder of the rent a car industry and president of Hertz. For five years Walter kept telling everybody he was going to go. He turned authority and responsibility over to his younger people and built up personal banking and real estate interests in his selected retirement locale—to soak up the energy that might otherwise tempt him to be a pest. When Walter retired neither he nor anyone else went into shock. And the company made new records.

Please don't underestimate the destructive potential of the retired chief executive who remains on the premises as a "consultant" or Chairman of the Finance Committee. If you are stuck with a predecessor who has contractual rights to an office and a secretary, insist that he be physically located someplace else. You can afford to rent him a handsome suite. Otherwise neither you, nor he, nor anyone else will know who's in charge.

BUDGETS

... must not be prepared on high and cast as pearls before swine. They must be prepared by the operating divisions.

Since a division must believe in the budget as its own plan for operations, management cannot juggle figures just because it likes to. Any changes must be sold to the division or the whole process is a sham.

Statements comparing budget to actual should be written not in the usual terms of higher (lower) but in plain English of better (or worse) than predicted by the budget. This eliminates the mental gear changes between income items (where parens are bad) and expense items (where parens are good). This way *all* parens become bad, and reports can be understood faster.

Most lenders, directors, and owners look at the monthly report to see if you made your budget. If you did, into the file with it. If you didn't, the report goes to an uninformed nitpicker who dreams up a lot of stupid questions. To save yourself this agony, put some arbitrary safety factor into the top statements that go outside the company. You haven't distorted the figures by which you and your managers are trying to measure trends, but you have something you can use to offset unforeseen setbacks without missing the budget as far as your investor/lenders are concerned.

C CALL YOURSELF UP

When you're off on a business trip or a vacation, pretend you're a customer. Telephone some part of your organization and ask for help. You'll run into some real horror shows. Don't blow up and ask for name, rank, and serial number—you're trying to correct, not punish. If it happens on a call to the Dubuque office, just suggest to the manager (through channels, dummy) that he make a few test calls himself.

Then try calling yourself up and see what indignities you've built into your own defenses.

CHAIRMAN OF THE EXECUTIVE COMMITTEE

Most companies are doing it all wrong. They're wasting this title (and others like Vice-Chairman or Chairman of the Finance Committee) on retired brass. Just because no one has the guts to tell old Mr. Leatherhead (our founder) that now's the time for him to go take those scuba lessons he always wanted.

These titles can be very useful.

A certain national institute was created recently. It had a young director with a good deal of experience in the field, but not much experience in managing an organization. He had his objectives clearly thought out and budgets prepared showing how and where he hoped to reach them, and what it would mean to the industry. But it was already clear that one of his problems was going to be visits and phone calls from international visiting firemen and from people in the industry wanting to talk to the boss.

He had no room in his budget for an assistant and besides people won't be pushed off on an assistant. He *did* have a substantial expense account for entertainment. So he called up an old friend who was retired and said, "I can't pay you a salary, but if you'll come in and take all these phone calls and lunches and dinners off my back, I'll make you Chairman of the Executive Committee. You can have some fun and meet some interesting people. And I can spend full time getting the institute going."

The key is the title. Nobody knows what it means. Bob Woodruff ran the Coca-Cola Company as Chairman of the

Executive Committee. It can mean much or nothing. But nobody ever gets mad when the boss says, "Let me switch you to the Chairman of our Executive Committee—this is the kind of thing he takes charge of."

In a business context, I've seen this work in an area like customer complaints. People who write or call with complaints want someone to listen, sympathize, apologize, and, if indicated, correct the matter. And the higher up their complaint is handled, the quicker their fire goes out. But companies still insist on having these complaints handled by "customer-service departments" or "complaint departments" or "adjustment departments." If I'm switched to one of those, I'm twice as mad as when I called. But I'm docile as a lamb if I hear, "Let me switch you to the Chairman of the Executive Committee. One of his people will take care of you. He likes to hear about all the complaints." I could be talking to the same clerk in the same department (except he is now speaking for the Chairman of the Executive Committee). And the letter of apology on that glorious letterhead not only rubs out my grievance, but retains me as customer and gives me something to brag about to your other prospects.★ The Russians have the best system. The real head of their typical embassy is a third assistant attaché, who is completely free of social obligations and can therefore devote himself fully to running the operation, while the French, British, German, and American ambassadors exhaust themselves on the cocktail- and dinner-party circuit.

★ If you are worried about the quality of the letters, ask them to send you blind copies—but not hold up the letters for your reaction. You must be careful not to nitpick. If the letters are substandard, rewrite the worst ones and keep your drafts until you have a dozen or so. Then go in and discuss yours compared with theirs. They'll appreciate the help and their letters will improve.

COMPROMISE AND KING SOLOMON

Compromise is usually bad. It should be a last resort. If two departments or divisions have a problem they can't solve and it comes up to you, listen to both sides and then, unlike Solomon, pick one or the other. This places solid accountability on the winner to make it work.

Condition your people to avoid compromise. Teach them to win some battles, lose others gracefully. Work on the people who try to win them all. For the sake of the organization, others must have a fair share of victories.

When you give in, give in all the way. And when you win, try to win all the way so the responsibility to make it work rests squarely on you.

COMPUTERS AND THEIR PRIESTS

First get it through your head that computers are big, expensive, fast, dumb adding-machine–typewriters. Then realize that most of the computer technicians that you're likely to meet or hire are complicators, not simplifiers. They're trying to make it look tough. Not easy. They're building a mystique, a priesthood, their own mumbo-jumbo ritual to keep you from knowing what they—and you—are doing.

Here are some rules of thumb:

1. *At this state of the art, keep decisions on computers at the highest level. Make sure the climate is ruthlessly hard-nosed about the practicality of every system, every program, and every report.* "What are you going to do with that report?" "What would you do if you didn't have it?" *Otherwise your programmers will be writing their doctoral papers on your machines, and your managers will be drowning in ho-hum reports they've been conned into asking for and are ashamed to admit are of no value.*
2. *Make sure your present report system is reasonably clean and effective before you automate. Otherwise your new computer will just speed up the mess.*
3. *Rather than build your own EDP staff, hire a small, independent software company to come in, plan your computer system, and then get out. Make sure they plan every detail in advance and let them know you expect them to meet every dollar and time target.*

Systems are like roads. Very expensive. And no good building them until you know exactly where they're going to wind up.

4. *Before you hire a computer specialist, make it a condition that he spend some time in the factory and then sell your shoes to the customers. A month the first year, two weeks a year thereafter. This indignity★ will separate those who want to use their skills to help your company from those who just want to build their own know-how on your payroll.*

5. *No matter what the experts say, never, never automate a manual function without a long enough period of dual operation. When in doubt discontinue the automation. And don't stop the manual system until the* non-experts in the organization think that automation is working. I've never known a company seriously injured by automating too slowly but there are some classic cases of companies bankrupted by computerizing prematurely.*

★ Everybody including the chief executive had to go through the Avis rental-agent training school. I once saw the Ph.D. who was responsible for all Avis systems panic and run from an O'Hare rental counter at the approach of his first real customer.

CONFERENCE BOARD: WHAT OTHERS DID, DON'T

The National Industrial Conference Board is a sophisticated center of research on yesterday. A nonprofit organization, it is paid by its member business organizations according to size or profit. Any conventional company can join.

NICB publishes all sorts of data about corporate practices. I've found it a valuable source for ideas—on what *not* to do.* When the vast majority of big companies are in agreement on some practice or policy, you can be fairly certain that it's out of date. Ask yourself: "What's the opposite of this conventional wisdom?" And then work back to what makes sense.

Editor's Note: This chapter is one of only two that Townsend did not include in Further Up the Organization. *(The other is "Office Hours.") Despite what he says in this chapter, Townsend may have later changed his opinion of the Conference Board. Appendix A is the text of a speech he delivered to the members of the organization in the 1970s.*

---

* A few titles from the 1969 index of NICB publications will give you the idea:
a) "The Board Chairman—Positions and duties. A job description is included." From this came the conviction that job descriptions are absurd for jobs above $150 a week.
b) "Human Relations—Personnel directors' responsibility for employee motivation ... 'Employee Motivation—What role for personnel?' " From this came the conviction that we don't need a personnel department at all.
c) "Committees—Use of committees in developing policies." From this came the conviction that you should liquidate all permanent committees.
d) "Executives—Fringe benefits. Special fringe benefits, such country-club memberships and chauffeurs to attract and hold top executives." From this came the conviction that you shouldn't have any of this nonsense paid for by the company.

CONFLICT WITHIN THE ORGANIZATION

... a sign of a healthy organization—up to a point. A good manager doesn't try to eliminate conflict; he tries to keep it from wasting the energies of his people (*see* Compromise and King Solomon; Memorandum, the Last; Salary Review: Annual Encounter Group).

Conviction is a flame that must burn itself out—in trying an idea or fighting for a chance to try it. If bottled up inside, it will eat a man's heart away.

If you're the boss and your people fight you openly when they think you're wrong—that's healthy. If your men fight each other openly in your presence for what they believe in—that's healthy. But keep all the conflict eyeball to eyeball (*see* Memorandum, the Last).

CONTACTS

A lesson very few have learned: If you want to approach the head of XYZ Corporation, call him cold. Tell him who you are and why you want to talk to him. A direct and uncomplicated relationship will follow.

The common mistake is to look for a mutual friend—or a friend's friend on his board, in his bank or investment bank or law firm—to introduce you. This starts all sorts of side vibrations and usually results in a half-assed prologue by the intermediary, who is apt to grind both edges of his own ax.

CONTROLLERS AND ACCOUNTING

No accounting system is very good, and all of them are infinitely variable. What the controller should do is insist that management pick one system and then not let them change it. He must be very strong on this point. Otherwise the management will fall or leap into the trap of inconsistency. The easiest way to do a snow job on investors (or on yourself) is to change one factor in the accounting each month. Then you can say, "It's not comparable with last month or last year. And we can't really draw any conclusion from the figures."

In a profit squeeze, management will come up with very creative reasons for changing the accounting system. They may even call on the outside accountants for support: "Isn't this better?" "Yes, that's better." But the point is: Is it a change? If it is, don't let them make it. This rule does not apply to the *very* occasional changes *originated* by the controller to show a more honest picture.

The controller will frequently be asked for figures in a hurry. He must never lose his head—that's what managements do, not controllers. If he does prepare a hurried report, he should label it for what it is: "Prepared under pressure and not understood."

The point is that if management wants to destroy its credibility with investors and with itself by preparing quickie projections and fearless forecasts, let it do so. But any report signed by the controller should be understood and believed honest (conservative) by the controller before he releases it. The controller's job is to see that all future surprises are pleasant.

The controller should never lose sight of his function: to provide an honest notation system by which managers can take responsible action toward their chosen goals and measure their progress. Honest reports are antibureaucratic; they give everybody a common starting-point from which to argue and make decisions.

A strategy meeting is apt to generate more heat than light unless everybody is talking from a common set of numbers.

The controller must not prepare or perpetuate reports for the Smithsonian archives. If his reports aren't useful to the line managers, they shouldn't be prepared.

From management's side, the important thing about getting the most out of the controller is to tell him about plans enough in advance so he can provide his input. Controllers are professionals. They don't gossip. Treat them as full members of the inner council. Save lots of agony by letting the controller have a good look at new ideas before they're implemented. If controllers are elected to insidership, they'll be valuable. If they're treated like plumber's helpers, they'll get their kicks making ends instead of means out of their reports and their systems—and you can't blame them. Yes, Virginia, accountants *are* people.

There abideth accuracy, timeliness, understanding, and unflappability in the controller's office—and the greatest of these is all four of them.

CONVICTION VS. EGO

Things get done in our society because of a man or a woman with conviction.

Bill Bernbach, when he was building the most exciting advertising agency of his time, had a round conference table in his office. He tried the customary rectangular one, but, as he said, "The junior men always sat at the foot and I sat at the head, and I learned that the light of conviction is often in the eyes of the junior men. With a round table, I was closer to them and less likely to miss it."

At the other extreme the economy is crowded with giant institutions—scientific, religious, educational, or artistic—that are not centers of conviction but monuments to an ego. There is probably one in your neighborhood. I have several in mind. Lots of money goes into them. Lots of good people work there. No results.

Before you commit yourself to a new effort, it's worth asking yourself a couple of questions: "Are we really trying to do something worthwhile here?" "Or are we just building another monument to some diseased ego?"

D DECISIONS

All decisions should be made as low as possible in the organization. The Charge of the Light Brigade was ordered by an officer who wasn't there looking at the territory.

There are two kinds of decisions: those that are expensive to change and those that are not.

A decision to build the Edsel or Mustang (or locate your new factory in Orlando or Yakima) shouldn't be made hastily; nor without plenty of inputs from operating people and specialists.

But the common or garden-variety decision—like when to have the cafeteria open for lunch or what brand of pencil to buy—should be made *fast*. No point in taking three weeks to make a decision that can be made in three seconds—and corrected inexpensively later if wrong. The whole organization may be out of business while you oscillate between baby-blue or buffalo-brown coffee cups.

DELEGATION OF AUTHORITY

Many give lip service, but few delegate authority *in important matters*. And that means all they delegate is dog-work. A real leader does as much dog-work for his people as he can: he can do it, or see a way to do without it, ten times as fast. And he delegates as many important matters as he can because that creates a climate in which people grow.

Example: An important contract with a supplier comes up for renewal. There is your present supplier and a major competitor. How many managers would delegate that decision? You're right: none. But you should. Here's one way:

1. *Find the man in your organization to whom a good contract will mean the most. (Can't be more than two levels below you—there's that bloody organization chart getting in the way.)*
2. *Take the pains to write out on one sheet of paper the optimum and the minimum that you expect from each area of the contract.*
3. *Give your organization (including John—the man you've picked to negotiate) a couple of days to discuss your outline, edit, subtract, delete, add, and modify. Then rewrite it, call John into the office (with his boss if there is one between him and you—I assume he's in favor of this or forget it).*
4. *With John on an extension, you phone the top man involved at each supplier, and after the amenities, you say: "This is John. I've asked him to negotiate this contract. Whatever he recommends, we'll do. There is no appeal over his head. I want a signed contract within thirty days."*

Now, I know that ninety-nine out of a hundred managers won't take this risk. But is it a risk? John is closer to the point of use. He will be most affected by a bad contract. He knows how much the company gains or loses by a concession in each area (and they know he does). And he'll spend full time on it for the next thirty days. Would you? I maintain the company will get a more favorable contract every time.

Note that you've given maximum authority and accountability to John. And you've been fair to (and put great pressure on) your suppliers by telling them the rules in advance.

Another example: Take two kinds of executives. Fred operates in the traditional way with his legal department. Some contracts he reads carefully and blue-pencils. Others he returns with a question (implying he has read carefully). Some he just signs. There is a feeling among his lawyers that Fred reviews the documents anyway, so occasionally they get sent upstairs right from the typewriter.

Bill's approach is different. He has said to his general counsel: "I don't want to read any legal documents covering transactions I've approved. If I have to sign them, then you initial them for legal aspects, and get the affected division or department head to initial for operating aspects. But remember, if you send it in with those two sets of initials, I'll sign it without reading it."

It seems to me Bill's way places the accountability where it belongs and protects the shareholders better without increasing the legal expenses. It also eliminates a lot of bulky papers that should never get in the chief executive's briefcase anyway.

DIRECTORS, BOARD OF: THE BACK-SEAT DRIVERS

The huge, successful company is a dinosaur, but it has one decisive advantage over the middle-size outfit that's trying to grow public; also over the established company that's in trouble enough to be ready for change. The advantage: most big companies have turned their boards of directors into non-boards. The chief executive has put his back-seat drivers to sleep.

This achievement has to be understood to be admired. In the years that I've spent on various boards I've never heard a single suggestion from a director (made *as* a director *at* a board meeting) that produced any result at all.

While ostensibly the seat of all power and responsibility, directors are usually the friends of the chief executive put there to keep him safely in office. They meet once a month, gaze at the financial window dressing (never at the operating figures by which managers run the business), listen to the chief and his team talk superficially about the state of the operation, ask a couple of dutiful questions, make token suggestions (courteously recorded and subsequently ignored), and adjourn until next month.

Over their doodles around the table, alert directors spend their time in silent worry about their personal obligations and liabilities in a business they can't know enough about to understand. The danger is that their consciences, or fears, may inspire them now and then to dabble, all in the name of responsibility.

Two simple tactics have been devised and time-tested in large organizations to head off this threat.

First, make sure that the board is composed partly of outsiders and partly of officers. Since all the important questions relate to the performance of key men and their divisions, no important questions will be asked. To do so would be a breach of etiquette, an insult to somebody at the table. Nor will any officer-director with an instinct for self-preservation (and a modicum of respect for the ignorance of the outside directors) ever bring a new or controversial idea before the board.

Second, be sure to serve cocktails and a heavy lunch before the meeting. At least one of the older directors will fall asleep (literally) at the meeting and the consequent embarrassment will make everyone eager to get the whole mess over as soon as possible. Caution: let sleeping directors lie. If one ever finds out that you rely on his somnolence, he will come to life with fierce and angry energy.

Unfortunately, smaller/newer companies often have directors who are investors or lenders able to exert the power of ownership. These directors are generally disastrous in their effect upon young managements. If not firmly under the thumb of the chief executive, they indulge a nervous impulse: they keep pulling up the flowers to see how the roots are growing.

Directors and the like (*see* Management and "Top" Management) spend very little time studying and worrying about your company. Result: they know far less than you give them credit for. What they know you can get best by a phone call. It is dangerous to take their formal advice seriously, or be too earnest about their casual questions. If they can ask important questions that the chief executive hasn't already thought of, he ought to be replaced.

Directors have one function, other than declaring dividends, which is theirs to perform: they can and must judge the chief executive officer, and throw him out when the time comes.★ So the manager of a small/new company must come to these terms: he must make it clear from the outset that he accepts without question the right of the directors to assemble whenever they want and decide to replace him.

Having in effect signed a resignation datable at their pleasure, he must meet with them quarterly for a whole day and report to them on the state and trend of the business. These four meetings and the monthly statements should enable the directors to judge him and fulfill their one significant function when the time comes.

Replacements for retiring directors should be other chief executives in completely unrelated businesses or experts active in related fields of knowledge. But suppliers of goods and services—like lawyers, accountants, bankers and investment bankers—should be kept off the board if at all possible. Give one of these a seat, and you shut off healthy competition from his profession to serve your company.

★ Since this task is painful, it is rarely performed even when all the directors know it is long overdue.

DISOBEDIENCE AND ITS NECESSITY

A commander in chief [manager] cannot take as an excuse for his mistakes in warfare [business] an order given by his minister [boss] or his sovereign [boss's boss], when the person giving the order is absent from the field of operations and is imperfectly aware or wholly unaware of the latest state of affairs. It follows that any commander in chief [manager] who undertakes to carry out a plan which he considers defective is at fault; he must put forward his reasons, insist on the plan being changed, and finally tender his resignation rather than be the instrument of his army's [organization's] downfall.

—NAPOLEON, Military Maxims and Thoughts

E EJACULATION, PREMATURE

If you discovered how to eliminate air pollution for $1.50 per state, the worst way to accomplish it would be to announce your discovery. You'd be amazed at how many people would oppose your scheme. The best way, if you could stay alive and out of jail, would be just to start eliminating it, state by state.

To get something done involving several departments, divisions or organizations, keep quiet about it. Get the available facts, marshal your allies, think through the opponents' defenses, and then go.

A premature announcement of what you're *going* to do unsettles potential supporters, gives opponents time to construct real and imaginary defenses, and tends to ensure failure.

It's a poor bureaucrat who can't stall a good idea until even its sponsor is relieved to see it dead and officially buried.

EMPLOYMENT CONTRACTS AND WHY NOT

To the company they say, "We've got him locked in, so we don't have to worry about him or listen to him as much as if we didn't."

To the individual they say, "Here's a date when your loyalty expires. Start thinking well in advance on what terms you'll renew."

Without employment contracts, the company must keep the climate challenging and invigorating and the rewards commensurate with the performance. Contracts in my opinion usually lose the men they are designed to hold. And keep those who have no other basis for staying. At the root of the disaster in American education today is the tenure system— whether of those non-teaching professors at Berkeley or of Al Shanker's lard-assed civil servants in Brooklyn. And don't think the kids don't know it.

Editor's Note: Albert Shanker (1924–1997) became president of the United Federation of Teachers in 1964 and was later president of the American Federation of Teachers. He was a controversial and powerful figure; the post-apocalyptic premise of Woody Allen's Sleeper *is that "a man named Albert Shanker got hold of a nuclear device."*

EPAULETS FOR THE CHIEF EXECUTIVE

With any encouragement some people in your company will spend full time getting the chief executive decorated by foreign governments. Or putting his picture in the papers, getting him made man-of-the-year by the American Pizza Association, or press-released by that new adventure in egomania, the American Academy of Achievement. A good chief executive will knock off all the nonsense. A weak one will accept the kudos because his indifferent performance as chief executive creates in him a real need for ego massage. Watch for the signs. Then you'll know what kind of chief executive you have—or are.

Editor's Note: The Academy was founded in 1961 and continues to hold an annual "Achievement Summit." It has bestowed its highest honor on such business leaders as Enron's Kenneth Lay and Drexel Burnham Lambert's Michael Milken.

EXCELLENCE: OR WHAT THE HELL ARE YOU DOING HERE?

If you don't do it excellently, don't do it at all. Because if it's not excellent it won't be profitable or fun, and if you're not in business for fun or profit, what the hell are you doing here?

EXCUSES

When you get right down to it, one of the most important tasks of a manager is to eliminate his people's excuses for failure. But if you're a paper manager, hiding in your office, they may not tell you about the problems only you can solve. So get out and ask them if there's anything you can do to help. Pretty soon they're standing right out there in the open with nobody but themselves to blame. Then they get to work, then they turn on to success, and then they have the strength of ten.

EXPENSE ACCOUNTS: THEORY X DISEASE

Like everything else you do—keep your expense account honest. Even if others are cheating openly. Not because you might get caught, but because honesty has to start somewhere. The people who are buying clothes or having their shirts laundered on their expense accounts are getting their fun that way because they're in a Theory X (*see* People) environment and can't get healthy kicks during office hours.

The typical response of a Theory X company to this game is to hire more people to write regulations and check the resulting paperwork. This costs more than the cheating, which, of course, doesn't stop—it just gets more inventive.

The real solution: repeal the regulations, fire the checkers, and start to build a Theory Y company (*see* People).

F FAIRNESS, JUSTICE, AND OTHER ODDITIES

Fairness, justice, or whatever you call it—it's essential and most companies don't have it. Everybody must be judged on his performance, not on his looks or his manners or his personality or who he knows or is related to.

Performances are distributed along the normal bell-shaped curve; a few outstanding ones at one end, the vast majority of satisfactory ones in the middle, and a few undeniably lousies at the other end.

Rewarding outstanding performance is important. Much more neglected is the equally important need to make sure that the underachievers *don't* get rewarded. This is more painful, so doesn't get done very often.

You never know who is reacting to what part of your effort to be fair. Some may flee the stick and some are drawn to the carrot. It's your job to create a system that's fair.★ And that's not easy. Injustice is built into our society and even into our instincts. To paraphrase Dwight Morrow, the world seems to be divided into those who produce the results and those who get the credit.

★ For some thoughts on keeping the President's salary fair, *see* President's Salary (Is He Really Worth $250,000?).

FAMILY BAGGAGE

The worst wives (from the standpoint of the effect on their husbands) in my experience are the overly ambitious ones. They seem to be constantly after their husbands to make more money. They don't understand that money, like prestige, if sought directly, is almost never gained. It must come as a byproduct of some worthwhile objective or result which is sought and achieved for its own sake.

Editor's Note: Townsend later revised this entry in Further Up the Organization *by changing "wives" to "company wives and husbands" and replacing "husbands" with "spouses."*

FIRING PEOPLE

Firing people is unpleasant but it really has to be done occasionally. It's a neglected art in most organizations. If a guy isn't producing after a year (two at most), admit that you were wrong about him. Keeping him is unfair to other people who must make up for his failure and untangle his mess. And it's unfair to him. He might do well in another company or industry.

Managers often duck this duty because it's unpleasant. But purging the bad performers is as good a tonic for the organization as giving sizable rewards to the star performers. Under profit sharing, you penalize the able by holding on to the inept.

Keep in mind that first impressions of performance are often wrong. There are slow starters who become stars, and flashes in the pan who sputter out.

Don't be needlessly cruel in firing someone. Figure out a reason that is true but enables him to preserve his ego. It is usually true that his combination of skills is not what's needed, or that the job is being restructured. If you don't feel compelled to destroy his self-regard, he can move on quickly without scars.

A good way to tell a line man from a staff man is to find out how many people he has personally fired. If only one or two, he may well be a staff man by nature. If put in a line position he may agonize for days over getting rid of some bad performer. He may hang on to one who clearly can't make it, or rig a transfer that puts a wounded, blood-hungry tiger into another part of the company. A good line man backs his gut feeling that Charlie is wrong for the job, fires him, and suffers a sleepless night or two. But the whole organization gets reinforced if he's right.

If you've inherited (or built) an office that needs a real house cleaning, the only sure cure is move the whole thing out of town, leaving the dead wood behind. One of my friends has done it four times with different companies. The results are always the same:

1. *The good ones are confident of their futures and go with you.*
2. *The people with dubious futures (and their wives) don't have to face the fact that they've been fired. "The company left town," they say. They get job offers, quickly, usually from your competitors who think they're conducting a raid.*
3. *The new people at Destiny City are better than the ones you left behind and they're infused with enthusiasm because they've been exposed only to your best people.*

G GEOGRAPHY, RESPECT FOR

If your business is in Cleveland, start or acquire an operation in Santa Barbara at your peril. Absentee management is fatal.

And the disaster potential is equal to the square of the distance—measured in hours—between your home base and the new plant. No matter how determined you are to visit it frequently, you'll discover that your capacity to find last-minute reasons not to go is unlimited.

If the new operation is in Europe or the Far East, the problems increase by cube functions. It is twenty-seven times harder to cope with an operation in Hong Kong than in Duluth.

GIFTS FROM SUPPLIERS

Right after Thanksgiving, put out the following memo in your own language and style:

There is nothing wrong with having personal friendships with representatives of those companies with whom we do business. However, this cannot be permitted to extend to the giving or receiving of gifts.

It is therefore against our policy for any employee to accept from any company or representative of a supplier company with whom we do or may do business any gifts of value, including cash, merchandise, gift certificates, weekend or vacation trips. This means, of course, returning any such gifts which may be delivered to your home or office.

Please see that the people within your area of responsibility are aware of this policy immediately.

Maybe people can keep two bottles of whisky or the equivalent. Anything more than that should be returned with thanks for the thought.

You can avoid embarrassing your friend the supplier by letting him read the memo. Swapping gifts is an insult to him and to you. It implies (1) that he's got to con you because he's cheating your company, and (2) that you're ready to accept the favor because you could make a better deal if you tried.

GOING A LITTLE BIT PUBLIC

Small privately owned businesses are tempted in hot stock markets to register with the SEC and sell a little stock.

Result One: The stock is quoted.

Result Two: The few employees and friends who own registered stock sell or buy a few shares a week and the stock moves!

Result Three: The company doesn't sell the 15-million-dollar convertible issue that is needed for solid expansion *("Gee, the stock is selling at 14 dollars a share—the company is worth 60 million dollars—why should we give away 40 per cent of it for 15 million dollars")*. Or management is afraid to shut down the perennial loss division *("It might hurt the price of the stock")*.

The valuation based on the tiny amount of stock traded is purely fictitious. But the mistakes made because of this purely paper value are costly. Sometimes deadly.

When André Meyer, senior partner of Lazard Frères, and I were talking about whether or not I'd run Avis for him, one of my requests (to which he readily agreed) was that neither of us would mention the price of the stock for two years. Most investment bankers, whose idea of a long-term investment is thirty-six hours, would never have agreed.

H HARVARD BUSINESS SCHOOL★

Don't hire Harvard Business School graduates. This worthy enterprise confesses that it trains its students for only three posts—executive vice-president, president, and board chairman. The faculty does not blush when HBS is called the West Point of capitalism.

By design, the "B-School" trains a senior officer class, the non-playing Captains of Industry. People who, upon graduation, are given a whirlwind tour of their chosen company and then an office and a secretary and some work to do while they wait for one of the top three slots to open up.

This elite, in my opinion, is missing some pretty fundamental requirements for success: humility; respect for people on the firing line; deep understanding of the nature of the business and the kind of people who can enjoy themselves making it prosper; respect from way down the line; a demonstrated record of guts, industry, loyalty down, judgment, fairness, and honesty under pressure.

I've already applied (no acknowledgment) for the job of guide to the Harvard Business School in 1995. By that time, tourists will be wandering around it like Stonehenge, asking, "I wonder what they used to do here?"

★ On page 372 of *The Age of Discontinuity,* Peter F. Drucker writes, "The business schools in the U.S., set up less than a century ago, have been preparing well-trained clerks. . . ." Peter, who is a good guy and shouldn't be judged by his pupils, ought to know. He teaches at NYU's business school.

Editor's Note: Townsend's prediction of Harvard's demise proved to be premature. The business school's endowment now approaches $2 billion, and the campus has expanded to forty-two acres, adding 325,000 square feet of new facilities in the 1990s. The president of the United States George Walker Bush is the first graduate of Harvard Business School to become commander-in-chief.

HEADHUNTERS

Occasionally (rarely, I hope) you may have to disregard the rule of 50 per cent (*see* Promotion, From Within) and go outside to fill an opening.

If you use a headhunter, go to the trouble of writing out your description of just the man you need (in your own words, not job-description boiler-plate). When he sends in a man for an interview, spend some time with him, even if at first glance he's not what you're looking for. Then call up your headhunter and tell him in some detail where he's on target and where he's off. Do this after each candidate. Pretty soon he'll zero in and start sending you the kind of people you want to choose from.

HUBRIS, THE SIN OF

Managers tend to make their biggest mistakes in things they've previously done best. In business, as elsewhere, hubris is the unforgivable sin of acting cocky when things are going well. As the Greeks tiresomely told us, Hubris is followed inexorably and inevitably by Nemesis.

I INCENTIVE COMPENSATION AND PROFIT SHARING

Editor's Note: Given the extensive use of financial figures throughout this entry, it may be useful to know that $1 in 1970 is roughly equivalent to $5 at the current writing. For example, the $15,000 salary Townsend mentions as a possible benchmark for incentive pay would translate into $75,000 today.

Some of this may not be applicable to your business, but the philosophy is.

To be effective, an incentive-compensation system of profit sharing should include the following characteristics:

1. *It should be related as directly as possible to performance. Therefore, wherever a participant has primary responsibility for a profit center his incentive compensation is directly related on a percentage basis to the profits of that center. Where his relationship is more remote, or where his judgments are of a staff type, evaluation is based on the judgment of his boss, but this is far less desirable.*
   ¶ *Spend company time and effort on the preparation of profit-and-loss statements for profit centers to enable as many people as practicable to be measured that way.*
   ¶ *Recognize that to have maximum effectiveness, profit-center-related bonuses must be computed in accordance with an accounting system which everyone understands and recognizes as fair. Therefore, all overheads should be brought down to the bottom line for bonus purposes on principles agreed to in advance. In order to*

avoid hours of hair-splitting, review the fairness every six months.
¶ *It is most desirable that a man be able to measure himself as he goes forward through the year, since he spends more time with himself than his boss does. Therefore his percentage of profits must be agreed to in advance.*

¶ *For maximum effectiveness, no ceiling should be put on a profit-measured bonus merely because it has become substantial. On the other side of the same idea, don't let any paternalistic feeling ameliorate the situation of a manager whose business has turned bad and who, for the first time, may receive no bonus at all.*

2. *Employees who do not have sufficient funds to support their reasonable family needs are distracted from their efforts. Accordingly, attempt to have salary measure the job itself and provide enough money for reasonable living costs. Incentive compensation is to measure variations in performance.*

¶ *Within these principles, limit executive base salaries, particularly at the top. For companies up to $100 million sales or $10 million pre-tax net, the chief executive officer and his three or four key executives could all be within a $40,000–$50,000 top range with very little differential among them. It isn't necessary for the chief executive officer to be paid more than the other officers, any more than a professional football coach has to be paid more than the star players. It is, of course, necessary to have a chief executive officer.*

3. *Get your board of directors to establish in perpetuity (a moral binder) that 15 per cent of total pre-tax profit will be available for those eligible★ for incentive compensation. The perpetuity is important. Otherwise the finks will try to reduce it when it becomes sizable.*

★ Anyone who makes $15,000 *or* has other people reporting to him or her (supervisor of a key-punch shift for example might make $6000) could be eligible. In a very small organization (200 people or so) *everybody* should be eligible.

4. *Bonuses measured by profit centers are handled by formula. Changes in formula should be resisted.*

¶ *The determination of discretionary bonuses is critical and much more difficult.* Fairness and full disclosure are the two keys to making the system work. *With this in mind:*

(a) The performance of every employee with one year of service who is a candidate for bonus participation must be rated by his boss in one of three categories. It is extremely important to resist pressures to increase the number of categories because complication tends to defeat the effort to be fair. Any manager should be able to place each of his people easily in one of three categories, but it becomes much more difficult with five or six categories.

(b) Generally speaking, ratings fall in the classification of unsatisfactory, satisfactory, and outstanding. It is anticipated that approximately 10 per cent will be at each extreme. *Any manager whose records show that he has no "unsatisfactory employees" may have an explanation to give to his boss. Similarly one who has no "outstanding" employees over a lengthy period of time also has an explanation to give.*

(c) Once the ratings have been made, the determination of bonuses is a purely mechanical job. Each unsatisfactory employee is given a rate of zero and will receive no bonus check. Each satisfactory employee will receive X per cent of his base salary. Each outstanding employee will receive 2X per cent. Extraordinary cases of multiple X per cent are also added in. ★ *The bonus pool produced by the 15 per cent of profits is then divided by total weighted salaries to produce the necessary computation of X per cent. An example of how this system works: Assume a company with 3,000 employees, $100 million of sales, $10 million of pre-tax, pre-incentive compensation earnings. Fifteen per cent of $10 mil-*

★ When you get all through with the 0, X, and 2X ratings, you ask, "Is there anyone with a 2X rating whose performance belongs in a class by itself?" If there is a 3X or 4X performance, it is generally acknowledged by acclamation.

lion gives us a pool of $1.5 million available for incentive compensation. Assume 400 people are on incentives related to profit centers and their formula bonuses add up to $1 million. This leaves $500,000 for discretionary incentive-compensation payments. Assume 50 people are eligible (base salary of at least $15,000 or have other people reporting to them). Assume 4 are rated unsatisfactory (no bonus); 42 are rated satisfactory (X per cent of base salary), and 4 are rated outstanding (2X per cent of base pay). In this year assume no ratings higher than 2X.

DISCRETIONARY INCENTIVE COMPENSATION

Eligible Employees	Performance Rating		Aggregate Base Salary	Incentive Compensation	Per Cent of Base Salary
4	Unsatisfactory	(0%)			
42	Satisfactory	(X%)	$820,000	$426,000	52
4	Outstanding	(2X%)	71,000	74,000	104
				$500,000	

X, in this case, turns out to be 52 per cent.

There were 42 people with satisfactory ratings. Each will receive incentive compensation of 52 per cent of base salary. Four people were rated outstanding. Each will receive 104 per cent of base salary as incentive compensation. This is an important barrier to break through. It lets some people really taste blood.

¶ This system can be prostituted and become a means of overpaying fat cats at the top. The chief executive at Avis never received a higher rating than X per cent (satisfactory), and in one year received an unsatisfactory rating.★

★ I rated myself and then submitted the rating to the board of directors for approval. It was understood that they could lower but not raise the rating (*see* President's Salary [Is He Really Worth $250,000?]).

(d) The message is as important as the medium, which is only money. Accordingly, bonus checks are NEVER DISTRIBUTED *by the chief executive officer, except to those reporting directly to him. Each bonus check is physically handed to an employee by his boss and is accompanied by a conversation (hopefully a dialogue and not a monologue) about the amount of the check (or absence of check) and the reasons for the evaluation. The most important conversations are with the employees who get no bonus checks because at that time one gets their undivided attention.*

Certain philosophical and psychological conditions follow from a system of the kind described above.

1. *In an ordinary economic sense, all management people are "partners" and, as such, have a major stake in one another's achievements.*
2. *There is a tough-minded attitude toward "carrying old Joe or his nephew" since everyone in the bonus system is paying for a share of old Joe or his nephew. People tend to be fairly outspoken where their pocketbooks are concerned.*

At the risk of repetition and to avoid misunderstandings, one might state the things which are *not* built into this compensation philosophy:

1. *No "thirteenth month" type of bonus or profit sharing by which every employee simply gets an extra pay period during the year, unrelated to his performance. Such an arrangement is worse than no incentive-compensation system because it misleads the directors and shareholders into believing that there is an incentive-compensation system when in fact there is none.*

2. *No incentive compensation is paid to an employee who does not otherwise merit it because "he is counting on it." Such a payment is always injurious to the organization and other employees, since it tends to reinforce the meritless one in the practices which justified an unsatisfactory rating.*

3. *No penalizing an employee—who has conducted himself well and shown tangible results—because of the failure of others either above him or elsewhere in the organization. Even during loss years when the company as a whole doesn't earn money, a few outstanding managers will receive incentive compensation or profit sharing based upon the results of the area under their control.*

4. *No reducing the percentage participation of a manager because his bonus is "getting too high," since such fudging corrupts the entire system. Your stockholders should yearn to have all your incentive-compensation participants get four times their base pay in bonus.*

5. *There are no secrets. No private payroll, for example. Since at least 15 per cent of your employees should share in incentive compensation, it is very difficult to keep them in the dark about any expenditure with which they are unfairly burdened. Because all profit centers carry full overhead, unnecessary overhead items are known throughout the organization and vocally resented. Accordingly, your executive people should have none of the following items which would reduce bonuses and cause resentment:*
   a) *Directors' fees.*
   b) *Executive Committee members' fees.*
   c) *Company-paid luncheon, golf, country, or yacht clubs.*
   d) *Executive aircraft.*
   e) *Executive dining rooms or executive washroom.*
   f) *Chauffeur-driven vehicles.*
   g) *First-class air travel.*
   h) *Company-paid travel expenses for family members.*
   i) *Corporate philanthropy.*

Your people should be encouraged to earn as much bonus as they can and then spend it on clubs, limousines, other corporate luxuries, or save it, or give it to charity. However, the choice should be theirs. Don't ask your people to subsidize the ego of fat cats at the top.

INDIRECTION: DON'T NEGLECT IT

Whether you're working in the mailroom or running the whole show, you'll be more effective if you vary your attack on your problems and opportunities. You'll also have more fun, and be less of a bore.

Know how something disappears if you stare at it long enough? And if everybody knows you're going to shout when you stand up, they'll turn off their receivers.

Work can be approached obliquely as well as directly. This is why people should be allowed to work out their own office hours and vacation patterns. Everybody will have a different system of building up a head of steam and then releasing it.

There is a time for engagement and a time for withdrawal. A time to walk around the job. A time to contemplate it—and a time to just laugh at it.

INSTITUTION, ON NOT BECOMING AN

If you ever get a good Theory Y (*see* People) organization going, the problem becomes how to keep it that way.

One good plan is for the chief executive to insist that he *must personally* use every form in the company before it's installed. Like: requisition forms (for pencils, pads, or air tickets), long-distance-telephone-call forms, or personnel department forms. And his secretary can't fill in the form for him.

If some psychiatrist in the personnel department invents a new application form with a whole lot of questions like, "How did you feel about your mother?", before it gets used the chief executive has to fill it out ... completely. This will kill a lot of bad ideas early.

Related to this is a function that you might describe as vice-president in charge of anti-bureaucratization. He must have a loud voice, no fear, and a passionate hatred for institutions and their practices. In addition to his regular duties, it's his job to wander around the company looking for new forms, new staff departments, and new reports. Whenever he finds one that smells like institutionalization, he screams "Horseshit!" at the top of his lungs. And keeps shouting until the new whatever-it-is is killed.

Billy Graham has a man named Grady Wilson who yells "Horseshit"—however you say that in Baptist—at him whenever he takes himself too seriously. Perhaps that's one of the reasons the Graham organization has been so successful. I had a Chairman of the Executive Committee who used to blow a launch-caller at me.★ Every chief executive should find someone to perform this function and then make sure he can be fired only for being too polite. Since the leader must lead the battle against institutionalization, it's to the leader that you should look for early signs of losing the war. Is he getting confused about who's God? Polishing up the image instead of greasing the wheels? Preoccupied with the price of the stock? Listening to the public relations department? Short-tempered with honest criticism? Are people hesitating before they tell him? Is he avoiding risks? Playing it safe? Talking to only certain people? Invisible to the rank and file? Hasn't even met some of the new people? Saying the same old magic words but doing something different?

Heartbreaking, isn't it? But he's probably had his five or six years and it's time for a new leader (*see* Wearing Out Your Welcome).

★ I was also blessed with a colleague who would break me up every now and then with a top-secret epistle beginning along these lines: "Dear Jefe de Oro: With regard to your latest pronunciamento, if you say so, it will be my hourly concern to make it so. But before I sally forth in service of this your latest cause, I must tell you with deep affection and respect that you're full of shit again … etc., etc." These epistles batted about .900.

INVESTMENT BANKERS

Like other suppliers of services (CPA's, commercial bankers, cleaning ladies, and lawyers), investment bankers work better if they sense that you aren't married to them. You should try to keep at least one alternate waiting eagerly (or at least waiting) in the wings.

You do this by having a quarterly lunch or dinner with your alternate contact and by supplying him regularly with your monthly figures (if these people can't respect confidences, nobody can).

While working with your current lawyer or banker, you give him every opportunity to do a good job. You are entitled to expect excellence from him. If you don't get it over a period of time, you had best change firms. It is usually easier to change firms than to reshape a relationship that has gone sour (*see* Lawyers Can Be Liabilities).

INVESTORS: KEEPING THEM INFORMED

They can be a nuisance when things are going well, but a positive threat to the company's existence when things have been going badly.

Here's how Lazard Frères handled the problem of keeping themselves and other investors informed in one case of a company they controlled. After the monthly statements were released, a certain partner would phone and say he was arriving at company headquarters the following morning. On arrival, he would go into an office by himself with a list of all division and department heads who were expected to be at headquarters that day. If some had planes to catch, that was noted on his list. He called them in *one at a time* and asked them any questions he wanted (they had all seen the same monthly statements because they were circulated freely to them with the *caveat* that they not be discussed outside the company). If he asked a question that could be answered better by someone else on the list, the questionee might ask to see the list and then suggest: "Why not ask *him* that question?" Or in some cases the questionee would have a go at answering anyway. The chief executive was called in for his half hour or so just like the others. At the end of the day the Lazard partner left.

Within a week at the outside, a triple-spaced memo would arrive and be circulated rapidly to all the people who had been interviewed (or their deputies if they were out of town on that particular day). The report was corrected as to fact (not style) and then sent back to the Lazard partner the same day. He would have it typed up in final form and sent to the directors and investors.

Note that this process only took an hour or less a month from each manager at the company. Also, since everybody at the company who was interviewed read the whole memo, it was an excellent intra-company communications device.

Since the company had a chance to review and modify before it went to the investors, any promises or deadlines became doubly binding on the people who had made or set them.

Two things about this technique bear watching.

First, the same man always came every month. He never sent a substitute. So his knowledge and understanding of the company increased geometrically and his relationships with the individuals became easier and easier.

Second, he was an honest and fair reporter of what he found.

J JOB DESCRIPTIONS— STRAIT JACKETS

Great for key-punch operators and other jobs where the turnover is high and the work is largely repetitive.

Insane for jobs that pay $150 a week or more. Judgment jobs are constantly changing in nature and the good people should be allowed to use their jobs and see how good they are.

At best, a job description freezes the job as the writer understood it at a particular instant in the past. At worst, they're prepared by personnel people who can't write and don't understand the jobs. Then they're not only expensive to prepare and regularly revise, but they're important morale-sappers.

Editor's Note: Townsend's benchmark of $150 is approximately $750 in current dollars.

K KILLING THINGS, V.P. IN CHARGE OF

It's about eleven times as easy to start something as it is to stop something. But ideas are good for a limited time—not forever.★

If Curtis Publishing had had a good V.P. in charge of killing things, the *Saturday Evening Post,* which was a great idea for many years, would have been killed before it ate up all those careers and all that capital.

The internal-combustion engine should long since have been killed and replaced with some form of external-combustion (pollutionless) engine.

General Foods, the AFL-CIO, the Bureau of the Budget, and the Ford Foundation should make it a practice to wipe out their worst product, service, or activity every so often. And I don't mean cutting it back or remodeling it—I mean right between the eyes.

And just to give us all a glimmer of light at the end of the tunnel, how about making it a matter of law that the federal government for the next hundred years will have to kill two old activities for each new one they start?

★ Dr. Robert Sobel, Associate Professor of History at Hofstra University, says that the British created a civil-service job in 1803 calling for a man to stand on the Cliffs of Dover with a spyglass. He was supposed to ring a bell if he saw Napoleon coming. The job was abolished in 1945.

L LABOR UNIONS

. . . including civil service and the American Association of University Professors, are a bloody nuisance.

Unionism, say the most idealistic leaders, has deteriorated into a kind of industrial police force that also sells insurance. The labor movement is now a conservative bureaucracy that resists the creative change of the good manager.

If you don't have them, the best way to avoid them is to create a Theory Y environment (*see* People) where your people have a chance to realize their potential (and get recognition for their contribution) in helping the company reach its objectives.

If you already have unions, then deal with them openly and honestly. Abide by their rules. For example, be meticulous about explaining every new benefit to the delegate privately and well in advance. After all, you want your people (union or not) to have the best deal you can give them. Whether the union grabs the credit for each item is completely immaterial. Don't sell your people short—they know. And don't turn your people over to the union politician by refusing to initiate benefits on the theory that the union will demand more than you can offer anyway.

Editor's Note: When Townsend wrote this, nearly a third of American workers were unionized. By 2005, the membership rate in unions had declined to 12.5 percent.

LAWYERS CAN BE LIABILITIES

Getting good legal advice is a question of picking the right individual, not the right firm. Usually the best is a young lawyer on-the-make. Look for a partner, or an about-to-be partner, who hasn't yet brought in any new business.

A good lawyer will give you his home phone, will travel on weekends and work weekends when it's needed, and will carry the corporate seal in his briefcase.

Beware of the lawyer who talks Middle English or statutory paragraph numbers. Though the common law did start before Chaucer, and though Congress does number sections of its output, you need a lawyer to answer questions, not to show off the glories of his trade.

Lawyers take to politics like bears to honey. Other things being equal, try to pick lawyers who are active in politics—particularly if you hire local lawyers in your regional operations (*see* Washington, D.C., Relations with). The best ones won't try or be able to "fix" things. But they're great antennae. Once you're identified as their client their friends in local and state governments will often talk to them before taking action that affects you.

LEADERSHIP

To lead the people, walk behind them.

—LAO-TZU

True leadership must be for the benefit of the followers, not the enrichment of the leaders. In combat, officers eat last.

Most people in big companies today are administered, not led. They are treated as personnel, not people.

Something is happening to our country. We aren't producing leaders like we used to. A new chief executive officer today, exhausted by the climb to the peak, falls down on the mountaintop and goes to sleep.

Where are our corporate Ethan Allens and John Hancocks and Nathanael Greenes, to say nothing of our George Washingtons, Ben Franklins, and Thomas Jeffersons? If we had to get the modern equivalent of our Founding Fathers together today, the first thing they'd do is hire Cresap, McCormick, and Paget★ to write the Constitution for them.

I'm afraid leadership is becoming a lost art:

"Most hierarchies are nowadays so cumbered with rules and traditions, and so bound in by public laws, that even high employees do not have to lead anyone anywhere, in the sense of pointing out the direction and setting the pace. They simply follow precedents, obey regulations, and move at the head of the crowd. Such employees lead only in the sense that the carved wooden figurehead leads the ship."†

★ Their initials, some say, stand for "Christ! more people!"
† Peter and Hull: *The Peter Principle.* New York: Morrow; 1969.

How do you spot a leader? They come in all ages, shapes, sizes, and conditions. Some are poor administrators, some are not overly bright. One clue: since most people per se are mediocre, the true leader can be recognized because, somehow or other, his people consistently turn in superior performances.

"As for the best leaders, the people do not notice their existence. The next best, the people honor and praise. The next, the people fear; and the next, the people hate . . .

When the best leader's work is done the people say, 'We did it ourselves!' "★

Editor's Note: Cresap, McCormick, and Paget was a powerful management consulting firm formed in 1945. It merged with Towers Perrin in 1983.

★ From Lao-tzu.

M MANAGEMENT AND "TOP" MANAGEMENT

"Top" management (the board of directors) is supposed to be a tree full of owls—hooting when management heads into the wrong part of the forest. I'm still unpersuaded they even know where the forest is (*see* Directors, Board of: the Back-Seat Drivers). "Top" management is free-floating and, like Gulliver's flying island Laputa, only occasionally in touch* with the real world of the company they're supposed to direct.

In the giant companies, it's an Elysian field† where you put your old pros (and a few legacies) to get them out of the way of the young Turks and let them figurehead annual charity drives. It's a pleasant vague world of ceremony and ritual built around the regular board and committee meetings. The chief executive, if he wants to be effective, spends a token‡ amount of time eating lotus with these Mandarins.

When stripped of the pejorative "top," the word "management" to me means the chief executive officer and all others who have one or more people reporting to them. Their jobs as managers are fundamentally all the same.

---

* Ralph Cordiner, as a member of top management of G.E., really *didn't* know his people were conspiring to fix prices.
† Take the elevator to the thirty-fourth floor of the Time/Life Building in New York City. It's occasionally possible to walk all around it without seeing a living soul except for the two receptionists.
‡ Four board meetings a year are infinitely less wearing on your operating and accounting people than twelve.

The best managers think of themselves as playing coaches. They should be the first on the field in the morning and the last to leave it at night. They're available to their players seven days a week from 8 a.m. to 11 p.m. In the business context, being there on the scene and available is a simple necessity—an if-not-forget-it. Timing is everything. If the manager isn't there when he's needed—to supply the blessing or the go-ahead or the missing piece of a puzzle—his people will lose satisfaction, then interest and zeal.

A good manager is a blocking back whenever and wherever needed. No job is too menial for him if it helps one of his players advance toward his objective. How many times has a critical project been held up because there was no one around who could get someone out of bed, or type up a fresh draft, or run off some copies on the Xerox. A good manager carries his players' home phone numbers with him and has an understanding with them that, just as he is available to them until eleven o'clock any night so they are available to him on the same terms.

Like a good coach, he protects his players from unreasonable demands of the owners. In business, he identifies company objectives and gets his players to see them as their objectives. Then he gets "top" management to agree to the objectives. Once this is done, he is able to be hard-nosed with "top" management whenever they try to distract him or his players.

"Top" managements are easily panicked when the organization is having a lean year. If the chief executive doesn't calm them down they can blow hither and yon and hot and cold. Under these conditions they must be constantly and forcefully told off when they suggest something or try something that not only doesn't help the chief and his team, but actually sets them back.

A good★ "top" management should read the monthly reports, meet quarterly with the chief executive, and function as his sounding board. For these duties, they should be paid less than, not more than, key division and department heads. The Establishment in any field seldom earns its pay.

★ I must take it on faith that there are good "top" managements: I've just never seen one.

MANAGEMENT CONSULTANTS

The effective ones are the one-man shows. The institutional ones are disastrous. They waste time, cost money, demoralize and distract your best people, and don't solve problems. They are people who borrow your watch to tell you what time it is and then walk off with it.

Don't use them under any circumstances. Not even to keep your stockholders and directors quiet. It isn't worth it.

Many organizations who've been through it will react promptly, thoroughly, and effectively to the threat: "If you fellows don't get shaped up in thirty days so you're a credit to the rest of the company, I'm going to call in Booz, Allen."

MARKETING

"Marketing" departments—like planning departments, personnel departments, management development departments, advertising departments, and public relations departments— are usually camouflage designed to cover up for lazy or worn-out chief executives.

Marketing, in the fullest sense of the word, is the name of the game. So it had better be handled by the boss and his line, not by staff hecklers. Once or twice a year for three or four days the boss takes ten, twenty, or thirty of his key people, including some from the ad agency and the controller's office, away to some secluded spot. On average they spend twelve hours a day asking unaskable questions, rethinking the business (What are we selling? To whom? At what prices? How do we get it to him? In what form?), four hours a day relaxing and exercising, and eight hours a day sleeping. It's hard work. But more good marketing changes will come out of such meetings than out of any year-round staff department of "experts" with "marketing" signs on the door.

MARS, MAN FROM

In solving a complex problem, pretend that you are a Martian. Assume that you understand everything about Man and his Society—except what has been done in the past by other companies in your industry to solve this particular problem.

For example, when the Massachusetts Turnpike Authority was about to tear down the Avis headquarters in Boston, we asked ourselves, "Where would a man from Mars locate the headquarters of an international company in the business of renting and leasing vehicles without drivers?" The main criteria became clear: near active domestic and international airports, so we could go see our managers and they could get to us; and in a good accounting and clerical labor market. So we moved to Long Island between JFK and LaGuardia, while our larger competition isolated itself on the tight little island of Manhattan.

MEETINGS

Generally speaking, the fewer the better. Both as to the number of meetings and the number of participants.

There are several kinds of useful meetings. Here are a couple:

The Weekly Staff Meeting

Purpose: information, not problem-solving.

For: all division and department heads.

Takes place same time same place, like TV news.

Starts *on the dot no matter who's missing.*

Goes around the room: reports on problems, developments (a crossed wire is handled by Joe saying to Pete: "I'll see you after the meeting on that"). A number of people should and will say "Pass."

Ends on the dot (or sooner).

No attendance taken.

No notice of meeting sent in advance.

No stigma for non-attendance.

One-page minutes dictated, typed, *and* circulated the same day.★

Every six months have a secret ballot—"Do we *need* a weekly staff meeting?"

★ The chief ought to write this. In the worst companies, the chief's assistant-to does it, and undoes all the trust created by the meeting.

The Problem- (or Opportunity-) Focused Meeting

Shouldn't happen more than a few times a year after a company gets going. A good manager with a nose for when an important problem or opportunity is facing his group earns his salt by calling this meeting. In my experience it's really a series of meetings.

After the first session, some are against, some are for, some think it's all a waste of time. I usually try to pick out a well-respected operating man who is reasonably enthusiastic for the idea and pair him with an assistant controller. They are asked to come back in a week to report (orally) to the original group on whether the idea makes sense.

After this second meeting the idea is either pretty obviously major (so you can ask for a written detailed battle plan to be submitted by your two-man team at the end of another week) or you apologize to the group for wasting time.

Two Meetings Better Than One

Some people absorb ideas quickly from conversation; others respond better to written material. First reactions are best from some people; the next day they're not so sure. Other people shouldn't be rushed.

Once I had a very able and valuable associate who would get negative and defensive if pressed for a decision in the first meeting on anything. He taught me that if it's worth having one meeting on a matter, it's usually worth having a second meeting first thing the next morning. At the first you pick up the convictions of the quick reactors, and at the second you give equal time to the just-as-valuable convictions of those who should sleep on it.

MEMORANDUM, THE LAST★

Use them for dissemination of noncontroversial information. Write them to yourself to organize your thoughts. But keep in mind that a memo is really a one-way street. There's no way to reply to it in real-time, or to engage it in a dialogue. Murder-by-memo is an acceptable crime in large organizations, and a zealous user of the Xerox machine gun can copy down dozens of otherwise productive people. The small company cannot survive such civil war games.

When two of your departments or divisions start arguing by memo and copying you, call them in and make them swear never to write another memo on that subject. Then listen to both sides and if they won't work it out then and there, decide it (*see* Compromise and King Solomon). When the conflict between the State and Defense departments was at its peak, it was rumored that 20 per cent of the employees of each department were there just to throw memo grenades at the other.

Memos and all other documents should always bear dates and initials. One of my colleagues once spent a twelve-hour night working on an undated document which turned out not to be the current draft. Why he was not convicted of mayhem remains a mystery.

If I were ever again sentenced to run a bank, I promise you one of my first official acts would be to write a memorandum to everybody, beginning, "This is the last memorandum ..."

★ *"The letter killeth, but the spirit giveth life."*—St. Paul

MERGERS, CONGLOBULATIONS, AND JOINT FAILURES

Joint ventures are almost always bad. At worst, both parents neglect the stepchild in favor of their own. At best, one parent does all the work, but has to give up half the rewards and justifiably begins to feel cheated. The worst kind of joint ventures are those with a supplier-customer relationship between the parents and the joint venture. Someone always ends up being screwed. Do it by yourself if it's worthwhile, and don't do it at all if it's not.

Acquisitions and mergers are a necessary evil for some companies. Avoid them like the plague if you can. If you can't, set up a team separate and distinct from the operating management of your company to handle them. An underworked but talented President, Chairman, or Chairman of the Executive Committee plus a talented director from Wall Street make a good combination. Let them work directly with someone assigned by the controller. Make sure that all three understand:

1. *That the business will be run as if no acquisition or merger will ever happen, and*
2. *That no one (including the chief executive officer) will ever be disturbed until the deal is in the eleventh hour, and I mean 11:55.*

At that point, the chief executive, the affected divisions and departments, and the controller's office can drop everything for forty-eight hours and, having heard about the deal for the first time, either buy it or kill it. But they don't spend a minute a year on the myriad deals that fall apart on the way to the closing.★

If you have a good company don't sell out to a conglomerate. I was sold out once but resigned (*see* Disobedience and Its Necessity). Conglomerates will promise anything for your people (if your stock sells for a lower multiple of earnings and has a faster earnings growth rate than theirs), but once in the fold your company goes through the homogenizer along with their other acquisitions of the week, and all the zeal and most of the good people leave.

Two and two may seem to make five when a conglomerate is making its pitch, but from what I've seen they are just playing a numbers game and couldn't care less if they make zombies out of your people.

Don't expect lawyers or investment bankers to be objective about conglomerates. Visions of sugar plums dance through their heads at the mention of Gulf and Western.

Editor's Note: The conglomerate Gulf+Western was renamed Paramount Communications in 1989 and was later merged into Viacom.

★ Of course your acquisition team should disclose the existence of this veto power before any negotiations get serious. Then they won't be accused of bad faith if you kill a deal at the last minute.

MESSAGE TO CHIEF EXECUTIVES

Probably whenever Sitting Bull, Geronimo, and the other chiefs powwowed, the first topic of conversation was the shortage of Indians. Certainly today, no meeting of the high and the mighty is complete until someone polishes the conventional wisdom: "Our big trouble today is getting enough good people."

This is crystal-clear nonsense. Your people aren't lazy and incompetent. They just look that way. They're beaten by all the overlapping and interlocking policies, rules, and systems encrusting your company.

Do you realize that your people can't make long-distance calls without filling out a report? Do you know what they have to go through to hire somebody—or buy something? Stop running down your people. It's *your* fault they're rusty from underwork. Start tearing down the system where it has defeated and imprisoned them. They'll come to life fast enough. Be the Simón Bolívar of your industry. Olé!

MISTAKES

Admit your own mistakes openly, maybe even joyfully.

Encourage your associates to do likewise by commiserating with them. Never castigate. Babies learn to walk by falling down. If you beat a baby every time he falls down, he'll never care much for walking.

My batting average on decisions at Avis was no better than .333. Two out of every three decisions I made were wrong. But my mistakes were discussed openly and most of them corrected with a little help from my friends.

Beware the boss who walks on water and never makes a mistake. Save yourself a lot of grief and seek employment elsewhere.

MISTRESSES

It's interesting that otherwise competent businessmen, capable of budgeting a complex operation, can't figure out that the cost of maintaining two women is twice the cost of one plus certain fringes. An early symptom of the mistress is a sudden surge of creativity in an executive's expense account. I once had a personnel vice-president who had taken up with one of our executive secretaries. If it had been outside the company I wouldn't have minded unless it interfered with his work. But a personnel man with his arm around an employee is like a treasurer with his hand in the till.

Having nothing but persistent rumors to go on, I was dragging my feet until all of a sudden all the executive secretaries got a raise (Thank heavens, somebody said later, he wasn't sleeping with a key-punch operator). But how do you get proof? I'm against using shamuses. Finally it came to me. Suppose it were me. Suppose my boss called me in and told me I was fired and why. If I were innocent, I'd go off like a roman candle. If I were guilty, I'd sheepishly ask, "Who did you hear that story from?"

That afternoon I called him in and told him. He lowered his eyes and asked, "Who told you that story?" He was a good man. I helped him start again a little way from temptation in another company. When I cut all the executive secretaries back to their previous pay levels, not one raised the voice of righteous indignation.

MOONLIGHTING

Like sleeping around, it scatters energy. It usually means that the salary isn't enough to cover living expenses or the psychic income is below the subsistence line. If there's a lot of it going on, it may be a sign that the system has defeated the people again. If they can't release their spare energies toward your goals, they'll moonlight for somebody who doesn't have job descriptions and policy manuals.

MOVING THE HEAD OFFICE

Put one man in charge of the whole operation (let's say his name is U. Heep), and give him the following frame of reference:

1. *All executive offices (including the chief's) must be the same size (small) and furnished with the same basic furniture.*★
2. *Don't consult or listen to anyone inside the company (especially not the chief executive) on matters of taste or preference.*
3. *Hire whatever independent experts you really need. But don't ask for advice unless you intend to use it.*
4. *If the building is ready on time, works reasonably well, and the cries of outraged vanity and offended taste die out within thirty days, it will be named the Heep Building. If not, it will be named the Heep Memorial Building.*

The usual practice is to hire architects and decorators and have them report to a committee of tasteless slobs. After taking twice as long and costing three times as much, this method leaves you with one solid result: all your key people are now completely preoccupied with status symbols and have no time for their work.

★ As anyone knows who has ever moved a head office, it can be very expensive. From the standpoint of billing cycles and collection of receivables, two moves equal one fire. My concern with sameness of basic furniture is in deference to the timetable. Six months after the move, when the business is out of shock, give each officer the same budget for refurnishing and redecorating and let him run amok if he wants to. If someone feels that cushions on the floor, psychedelic posters, and black lights will help him get his job done, I'm all for it. For further philosophy on offices, *see* Telephone Operators.

N NEPOTISM, THE SMELL OF

The fatal fact about nepotism is that the really good people won't go to work for you in the first place or will quit or quit trying for your job when they spot your uncle, brother, nephew, wife, mistress, or son on the payroll. They can't expect a fair shake if you're getting breakfast news from a special source.

And what nepotists can't seem to understand is that it doesn't matter whether they're playing family favorites or not. Or even how good the relative is. If there's even a bare possibility that you're prejudiced, the smell of it will scare off or turn off the very people you need most. The stockholders will never know how many good people they missed who never applied for a job.

One odd thing about nepotism is that people with strong Calvinist tendencies are often hardest to persuade. The molecular biologist working long hours for low pay to cure cancer has his wife working as a lab technologist. When questioned, he says, "I'd have to pay twice as much for someone half as good." He misses the point. If she ever cuts a corner because she's thinking of the salad for dinner or the baby's formula, the rest of the lab staff will catch the infection. To them, she's the boss's wife.

"But my brother is the best salesman in the business," says the sales manager. Then let him prove it somewhere else. If he's that good, it's not fair to him to stay under you where he'll never know for sure how good he is.

Nepotism is a way of screwing the non-family shareholders. If all the shareholders are family, then it doesn't matter: they're only screwing each other. But when Ford Motor Company stock was sold to the public, Henry II and his brothers should have gotten out of the management. When they didn't, it seemed inevitable that their first classic misadventure should turn out to be named after a relative.

In the old world, nepotism worked fine for the Rothschilds. It won't work in the new world for anybody.

If the company's economic and financial position is weak, the results of nepotism can show up fast. Gerry Eskow succeeded his father as president of Yale Express in 1960. Five years later the company went bankrupt.

In rich companies built on an important share of an oligopoly, nepotism will take longer to work its woe.

But two or three more generations of Fords, Sarnoffs, and Watsons in charge may well suffice to kill Ford, RCA, and IBM just as dead as little Yale Express.

Editor's Note: Ironically, Robert Sarnoff did bequeath leadership of RCA to his son the year this book was written, although his son died unexpectedly a year later; Sarnoff returned to RCA, buying Hertz, Townsend's fiercest competitor while at Avis. Sarnoff was ousted in a boardroom coup in 1975, and the company was sold to GE in 1986. Thomas Watson Jr., who succeeded his father at IBM, retired in 1973. William Clay Ford Jr. gave up the title of CEO at Ford Motor Company in 2006 after years of losses and seeing Ford bond ratings fall to junk status. The bankruptcy of Yale Express Systems, a trucking company, was a news item at time of Townsend's writing.

NO-NO'S

Reserved parking spaces. If you're so bloody important, you better be first one in the office. Besides, you'll meet a nice class of people in the employees' parking lot.

Special-quality stationery for the boss and his elite.

Muzak, except in the areas where the work is only suitable for mental defectives.

Bells and buzzers (even telephones can be made to signal with lights).

Company shrinks. Unless it's really optional, and the shrink reports only to the patient, and suitable precautions have been taken to make sure the personnel department can't tap into the data.

Outside directorships and trusteeships for the chief executive. Give up all those non-jobs. You can't even run your own company, dummy.

Company plane. It's just a variation of the company-paid golf club, and the big office with three secretaries. Another line drawn through the company between the Brahmins and the untouchables. And the plane's always in Palm Beach, Augusta, Aspen, or Las Vegas when the business needs it. Best thing about it: if it has only one pilot, someday he'll get ptomaine with a whole load of "top" management aboard ...

Manager's Monthly. Or any other time-consuming report imposed on the troops by "top" management. It's a joke because it consumes ten pounds of energy to produce each ounce of misunderstanding.

Except in poker, bridge, and similar play-period activities, **don't con anybody.**

Not your wife
Not your children
Not your employees
Not your customers
Not your stockholders
Not your boss
Not your associates
Not your suppliers
Not your regulatory authorities
Not even your competitors

Don't con yourself either.

Social relations within the firm. Okay with your peers. But not with people who report to you. You'll inevitably see more of the ones you like—and they may not be the best performers. Your own performance depends on your ability to be just. Don't make it any tougher than it is.

Hiring. To keep an organization young and fit, don't hire anyone until everybody's so overworked they'll be glad to see the newcomer no matter where he sits.

Trade associations—as a chance to fix prices, and allocate customers and markets with your friendly competitors. Antitrust laws are different: you're not innocent until proven guilty. If all your customers are north of Main Street and all your competitor's customers are south of Main Street, you're both guilty by inference. And nobody has to prove the two of you ever communicated in any way. Treble damages. Jail. So watch it, bubele.

Conventions. The public relations dream: much money, time, and energy signifying nothing. The best way is to ignore them. The next best way is to send one line man (rotate the assignment like kitchen police). On his return, ask him to make a thirty-second all-inclusive oral report to the weekly staff meeting covering everything of significance that he heard, saw, and learned. The worst way is to give your P.R. department a blank check and tell them to make a big splash.

House organs. Spend the money making stockholders out of your employees and then sending them (along with the other stockholders) honest reports on how the company's really doing: good and bad. Reading a house organ is like going down in warm maple syrup for the third time.

Greed. To increase our share of the market a few years ago, I was on the verge of approving the start-up of a new subsidiary—which would compete with our bread-and-butter business—at discount prices. To verify my own brilliance I tried the idea out on a tall, rangy regional vice-president named Stepnowski. After hearing the plan described in some detail, he sank the whole project with one sentence: "I don't know what *you* call it, but we Polacks call that 'pissing in the soup.' "

O OBJECTIVES

One of the important functions of a leader is to make the organization concentrate on its objectives. In the case of Avis, it took us six months to define one objective—which turned out to be: "We want to become the fastest-growing company with the highest profit margins in the business of renting and leasing vehicles without drivers."

That objective was simple enough so that we didn't have to write it down. We could put it in every speech and talk about it wherever we went. And it had some social significance, because up to that time Hertz had a crushingly large share of the market and was thinking and acting like General Motors.

It also included a definition of our business: "renting and leasing vehicles without drivers." This let us put the blinders on ourselves and stop considering the acquisition of related businesses like motels, hotels, airlines, and travel agencies. It also showed us that we had to get rid of some limousine and sightseeing companies that we already owned.

Once these objectives are agreed on, the leader must be merciless on himself and on his people. If an idea that pops into his head or out of their mouths is outside the objective of the company, he kills it without a trial.

Peter Drucker was never more right than when he wrote: "Concentration is the key to economic results ... no other principle of effectiveness is violated as constantly today as the basic principle of concentration. . . . Our motto seems to be: 'Let's do a little bit of everything.' "★

★*Managing for Results.* New York: Harper & Row; 1964.

It isn't easy to concentrate. I used to keep a sign opposite my desk where I couldn't miss it if I were on the telephone (about to make an appointment) or in a meeting in my office: "Is what I'm doing or about to do getting us closer to our objective?" That sign saved me from a lot of useless trips, lunch dates, conferences, junkets, and meetings.

Most of all, work on simplifying and distilling your statement of objectives. Cato boiled his down to three words*— and by saying them over and over eventually wiped out the competition.

---

*Lest we forget, the words were: *Delenda est Carthago.*

OFFICE HOURS

Anyone who makes over $150 a week should be allowed to set his own office hours. Many will conform to the traditional nine to five but it should be *their* choice. A few will set hours that reduce their effectiveness and cost them their jobs. Overall it's worth it.

People have different metabolisms. If you work better from noon to midnight and your job makes those hours appropriate, you should be able to do it. And if you must have a secretary (*see* Secretary, Freedom from a) pick one with the same general metabolism.

Editor's Note: This 1970 weekly salary would translate into nearly $40,000 yearly salary in today's dollars. It is also worth noting that this is one of only two chapters in the first edition that was dropped from the 1984 edition.

OFFICE PARTY, HOW NOT TO DO THE ANNUAL

1. *Start it at 5 p.m. instead of noon, so the company doesn't lose any man-hours.*

2. *Invite spouses so bosses and their secretaries don't enjoy dancing together.*

3. *Make sure the top brass either doesn't show or puts in a token appearance—underscoring the difference between them and the rest of us.*

4. *Invite clients and suppliers to help reinforce their contempt for your company.*

5. *Skimp on the setting. A third-rate roadhouse is always good.*

6. *Cut corners on the food and booze. Two-day-old hors d'oeuvres left over from a wedding, a tray of Manhattans, and a mystery punch ought to do it.*

7. *Save money on the music. Better than a phonograph is a tin-eared accordionist whose idea of a new number is "I Could Have Danced All Night."*

8. *Kill two birds by combining it with the annual quarter-century-club party. Then all your employees can see living examples (you should excuse the expression) of what twenty-five years in your outfit will do to what were once healthy human beings.*

9. *Better yet, turn the whole thing over to the head of the personnel department and tell him to use his best judgment.*

ORGANIZATION CHARTS: RIGOR MORTIS

They have uses: for the annual salary review; for educating investors on how the organization works and who does what.

But draw them in pencil. Never formalize, print, and circulate them. Good organizations are living bodies that grow new muscles to meet challenges. A chart demoralizes people. Nobody thinks of himself as *below* other people. And in a good company he isn't. Yet on paper there it is. If you have to circulate something, use a loose-leaf table of organization (like a magazine masthead) instead of a diagram with the people in little boxes. Use alphabetical order by name and by function wherever possible.

In the best organizations people see themselves working in a circle as if around one table. One of the positions is designated chief executive officer, because somebody has to make all those tactical decisions that enable an organization to keep working. In this circular organization, leadership passes from one to another depending on the particular task being attacked—without any hang-ups.

This is as it should be. In the hierarchical organization, it is difficult to imagine leadership anywhere but at the top of the various pyramids. And it's hard to visualize the leader of a small pyramid becoming temporarily the leader of a group of larger pyramid-leaders which includes the chief executive officer.

The traditional organization chart has one dead giveaway. Any dotted line indicates a troublemaker and/or a seriously troubled relationship. It also generally means that an unsatisfactory compromise (*see* Compromise and King Solomon) has been worked out and the direct solution has been avoided.

P PEOPLE

There's nothing fundamentally wrong with our country except that the leaders of all our major organizations are operating on the wrong assumptions.* We're in this mess because for the last two hundred years we've been using the Catholic Church and Caesar's legions as our patterns for creating organizations. And until the last forty or fifty years it made sense. The average churchgoer, soldier, and factory worker was uneducated and dependent on orders from above. And authority carried considerable weight because disobedience brought the death penalty or its equivalent.†

From the behavior of people in these early industrial organizations we arrived at the following assumptions,‡ on which all modern organizations are still operating:

1. *People hate work.*
2. *They have to be driven and threatened with punishment to get them to work toward organizational objectives.*
3. *They like security, aren't ambitious, want to be told what to do, dislike responsibility.*

---

* By all the evidence, the other industrialized countries are as bad off, but no worse; their major institutions are operated on the same silly assumptions.
† Dismissal and blacklisting brought starvation to an industrial worker; excommunication brought the spiritual equivalent of death to a churchgoer.
‡ Douglas McGregor (*see* Bibliography) called these three assumptions "Theory X." Organizations that run on these premises—the hierarchies—are Theory X outfits.

You don't think we are operating on these assumptions? Consider:

1. *Office hours nine to five for everybody except the fattest cats at the top. Just a giant cheap time clock. (Are we buying brains or hours?)*
2. *Unilateral promotions. For more money and a bigger title I'm expected to jump at the chance of moving my family to New York City. I run away from the friends and a life style in Denver that have made me and my family happy and effective. (Organization comes first; individuals must sacrifice themselves to its demands.)*
3. *Hundreds of millions of dollars are spent annually "communicating" with employees. The message always boils down to: "Work hard, obey orders. We'll take care of you." (That message is obsolete by fifty years and wasn't very promising then.)*

Back off a minute. Let's pretend we know everything man knows about human nature and its present condition here, but nothing about man's organizations and the assumptions on which they're based. These things★ we know about man:

1. *He's a wanting animal.*
2. *His behavior is determined by unsatisfied needs that he wants to satisfy.*
3. *His needs form a value hierarchy that is internal, not external:*
   (a) *body (I can't breathe.)*
   (b) *safety (How can I protect myself from . . . ?)*
   (c) *social (I want to belong.)*
   (d) *ego (1. Gee, I'm terrific. 2. Aren't I? Yes.)*
   (e) *development (Gee, I'm better than I was last year.)*

Man is totally motivated by each level of need in order—until that level is satisfied. If he hasn't slept in three days he's

---

★ McGregor again.

totally motivated by a need for sleep. After he has slept, eaten, drunk, is safe, and has acceptance in a group, he is no longer motivated by those three levels of needs. (McGregor's examples: The only time you think of air is when you are deprived of it; man lives by bread alone when there is no bread.)

We know that these first three need levels are pretty well satisfied* in America's work force today. So we would expect man's organizations to be designed to feed the ego and development needs. But there's the whole problem. The result of our outmoded organizations is that we're still acting as if people were uneducated peasants. Much of the work done today would be more suitable for young children or mental defectives.

And look at the rewards we're offering our people today: higher wages, medical benefits, vacations, pensions, profit sharing, bowling and baseball teams. *Not one can be enjoyed on the job.* You've got to leave work, get sick, or retire first. No wonder people aren't having fun on the job.

So what are the valid assumptions for present-day circumstances? McGregor called them "Theory Y":

1. *People* don't *hate work. It's as natural as rest or play.*
2. *They don't* have *to be forced or threatened. If they commit themselves to mutual objectives, they'll drive themselves more effectively than you can drive them.*
3. *But they'll commit themselves only to the extent they can see ways of satisfying their ego and development needs (remember the others are pretty well satisfied and are no longer prime drives).*

All you have to do is look around you to see that modern organizations are only getting people to use about 20 per

---

* This book does not come to grips with the problem of America's 20 million poor: it deals with the 80 million psychiatric cases who do have jobs.

cent—the lower fifth—of their capacities. And the painful part is that God didn't design the human animal to function at 20 per cent. At that pace it develops enough malfunctions to cause a permanent shortage of psychoanalysts and hospital beds.

Since 1952 I've been stumbling around building and running primitive "Theory Y" departments, divisions, and finally one whole "Theory Y" company: Avis.

In 1962 after thirteen years Avis had never made a profit.* Three years later the company had grown internally (not by acquisitions) from $30 million sales to $75 million sales, and had made successive annual profits of $1 million, $3 million, and $5 million. If I had anything to do with this, I ascribe it all to my application of Theory Y. And a faltering, stumbling, groping, mistake-ridden application it was.

You want proof? I can't give it to you. But let me tell you a story. When I became head of Avis I was assured that no one at headquarters was any good, and that my first job was to start recruiting a whole new team. Three years later, Hal Geneen, the President of ITT (which had just acquired Avis), after meeting everybody and listening to them in action for a day, said, "I've never seen such depth of management; why I've already spotted three chief executive officers!" You guessed it. Same people. I'd brought in only two new people, a lawyer and an accountant.

Bill Bernbach used to say about advertising effectiveness: "Ninety per cent of the battle is what you say and 10 per cent is what medium you say it in." The same thing is true of people. Why spend all that money and time on the *selection* of people when the people you've got are breaking down from under-use.

Get to know your people. What they do well, what they enjoy doing, what their weaknesses and strengths are, and what

---

* Except one year when they jiggled their depreciation rates.

they want and need to get from their job. And then try to create an organization around your people, not jam your people into those organization-chart rectangles. The only excuse for organization is to maximize the chance that each one, working with others, will get for growth in his job. You can't motivate people. That door is locked from the inside. You *can* create a climate in which most of your people will motivate themselves to help the company reach its objectives. Like it or not, the only practical act is to adopt Theory Y assumptions and get going.

It isn't easy, but what you're really trying to do is come between a man and his family. You want him to enjoy his work so much he comes in on Saturday instead of playing golf or cutting the grass.

Theory Y is the explanation for Ho Chi Minh's unbelievable twenty-five-year survival against the mighty blasts of Theory X monsters of three nations:

There is nothing to distinguish their generals from their private soldiers except the star they wear on their collars. Their uniform is cut out of the same material, they wear the same boots, their cork helmets are identical and their colonels go on foot like privates. They live on the rice they carry on them, on the tubers they pull out of the forest earth, on the fish they catch and on the water of the mountain streams. No beautiful secretaries, no pre-packaged rations, no cars or fluttering pennants . . . no military bands. But victory, damn it, victory!★

★ Jules Roy: *The Battle of Dienbienphu*, New York: Harper & Row; 1965, p. 304.

PERSONNEL (PEOPLE VS.)

Fire the whole personnel department.

Unless your company is too large (in which case break it up into autonomous parts), have a one-girl people department (not a personnel department). Records can be kept in the payroll section of the accounting department and your one-girl people department (she answers her own phone and does her own typing) acts as personnel (sorry—people) assistant to anybody who is recruiting.★ She lines up applicants, checks references, and keeps your pay ranges competitive by checking other companies.

On the subject of pay ranges, I've long held the conviction that it's much less expensive to recruit from the top of the barrel by paying top wages. Yet many big personnel departments in insurance companies, banks, and the like, consciously recruit from the lower half of the barrel to "save money." If they only realized what they were doing to themselves.

The trouble with personnel experts is that they use gimmicks borrowed from manufacturing: inventories, replacement charts, recruiting, selecting, indoctrinating and training machinery, job rotation, and appraisal programs. And this manufacturing of men is about as effective as Dr. Frankenstein was. As McGregor points out, the sounder approach is agricultural. Provide the climate and proper nourishment and let the people grow themselves. They'll amaze you.

Editor's Note: Townsend later changed "one-girl" to "one-person."

★ The important thing about hiring is the chemistry or the vibrations between boss and candidate: good, bad, or not there at all.

PLANNING, LONG-RANGE: A HAPPENING

Planning is best handled by the boss and his key men (*see* Marketing, for how).

Once I was asked to head up a new long-range planning effort. My wife listened to my glowing description of my new job. Next evening she blew the whole schmeer out of the water by asking: "What did you plan today, dear?" Bless her.

POLICY MANUALS

Don't bother. If they're general, they're useless. If they're specific, they're how-to manuals—expensive to prepare and revise.

The only people who read policy manuals are goldbricks and martinets. The goldbricks memorize them so they can say: (1) "That's not in this department," or (2) "It's against company policy." The martinets use policy manuals to confine, frustrate, punish, and eventually drive out of the organization every imaginative, creative, adventuresome woman and man.

If you *have* to have a policy manual, publish the *Ten Commandments*.

P.R. DEPARTMENT, ABOLITION OF

Yes, fire this whole department, too. If you have an outside P.R. firm, fire them too.

Most businesses have a normal P.R. operation: press releases, clipping services, attempts to get interviewed; all being handled, as usual, by people who are embarrassingly uninformed about the company's plans and objectives.

We made many mistakes at Avis, but we were at least smart enough to realize that the professional P.R. operation was as dead as the button-hook industry. We knew too many editors had trigger mechanisms that acted automatically to wastebasket anything starting off: "For release."

So we eliminated the P.R. staff. And we called in the top ten or so people in the company and the telephone operators and told them they were the P.R. department.

The telephone operators were given the home phones of the ten people and asked to find one of them if any of the working press called with a question.

The ten people were given the following framework within which they could be themselves and talk freely:

1. *Be honest. If you don't know, say so. If you know but won't tell, say so.*
2. *Pretend your ablest competitor is listening. If he already knows your latest marketing plan, you use the call to announce it; if not, shut up. (This mind-set also prevents knocking the competition, which is always bad for everybody.)*

3. *Don't forecast earnings. If asked why not, tell them we don't do in public anything we can't do consistently well (and believe me, nobody can forecast earnings consistently well).*

This system worked well.* Example. One day Ford Motor Company announced they were going directly into the rent a car business through any Ford dealer that wanted to. The *Wall Street Journal* phoned and was put through to the general manager of our rent a car division. Next day the front-page left-hand column was heavily salted with quotes from their conversation.

Far down the page our competitor's V.P. of Public Relations had pulled off this coup: "A spokesman for the Hertz Corporation said they were studying the matter."

Hertz was older and twice our size, but who looked like the industry leader that morning?

---

* It also worked with security analysts and portfolio managers who wanted to come see us. When one telephoned for an appointment, I'd give him the rules: "Our next session [we had about one a month] is on April 10. It lasts from ten to four. There'll be three or four other analysts present. We'll give you our board room and you can call in whoever's around of our top ten people one at a time." Not one liked the idea at first. But each one admitted later that he'd learned from the other questions. And each had been impressed by the openness and competence of our people. Yet the time consumed by us was less than forty-five minutes per Avis man per month.

PRESIDENT'S SALARY (IS HE REALLY WORTH $250,000?)

Every couple of years at an otherwise routine board meeting, some outside director asks your chief executive to leave the room.★ Then he mumbles something about underpaid and proposes a raise to $250,000 a year, which is unanimously approved.†

During the months that follow, the chief proposes raises for his various top officers and when the process is complete, they are all nicely in line with each other and with the average relationship between top officers' salaries of all large, medium, or small corporations as compiled and published by the National Industrial Conference Board.

Over the years a sizable and unjustifiable salary gaposis develops between that privileged group and the people who are doing the real work.

Pick out the workers in your company whose knowledge or experience gets you from January to December. Which people could really hurt by going over to the competition? Your board of directors? Your vice-chairman? Hell, no! If they joined your competitor en masse, you'd be fourteen lengths ahead in a year, considering your lightened load, and your competitor's added burden.

★ Chances are your chief executive sits on his board and does the same for him.
† This whole procedure defies a sound principle: "Board meetings (or any other silly ritual) should be conducted as if Wilma Soss, the corporate gadfly, were present by invitation."

Your key resource people may be engineers, designers, artists, city managers, accountants, mathematicians, chemists, editors, district sales managers, or some of each. But average them all out and they're making one fifth of what the chief executive gets.

Fair? Not in my book. And it cuts two ways.

The salary gap makes the key people frustrated and restless. And as the chief's salary edges up out of the earth's atmosphere, one of two reactions sets in. Subconsciously or consciously impressed by how much he is paid, he either becomes:

1. *Arrogant (since I'm so good, I'd better see that all important decisions get the laying-on-of-hands in my office before they're made). The company grinds to a halt and the zeal drains out.*

or

2. *Timid (I'm paid this much to make sure nothing goes wrong: so I'd better have a look at everything before it happens). The company grinds to a halt and the zeal drains out.*

Why does the chief executive permit this gaposis, which is so bad for the company? I guess because he hasn't thought it through. It certainly can't be the money. He doesn't get to keep it. He's just a conduit between his own stockholders and the Internal Revenue Service.

Gaposis can be fought.

When André Meyer hired me to run Avis, the last item he covered was my salary. "You'll be paid $50,000."

"No I won't," said I. "As an about-to-be-substantial stockholder I insist the President be paid $36,000 because that's top salary for a company that has never earned a nickel for its stockholders."

"*D'accord,*" said André, who always knows when to give up.

When Avis moved into the black a year later, General Sarnoff, one of our outside directors, asked me to leave the room. "I'd prefer not to," I said.

"Why not?" he asked.

"Because if I do you'll raise my salary. And since I'm now overpaid* in relation to the service agents, rental agents, city managers, and regional vice-presidents who run this company, you'll be defeating my crusade for a just compensation system. And since 15 per cent of the pre-tax profits goes into a profit sharing fund for the top five hundred people, that raise will come out of their pockets, and if I were them I wouldn't stand for it."

The General never liked to be crossed and I'm not sure he ever forgave me. But he learned so much about the rent a car business on the Avis board that soon after Avis was sold to ITT, he bought Hertz for RCA. Come to think of it, we should have charged him tuition fees.

Ideally, a new chief executive should negotiate his own compensation on a once-and-for-all basis before he goes to work. That is, he may get fired at any time, but if things go well, he gets no more goodies except those that flow from the success of the enterprise (stock appreciation, for example). This puts him in the position of dividing the spoils objectively among his teammates. If he is the divider and a recipient, his directors and stockholders will usually prevail on him to allocate himself more than he deserves.

Editor's Note: In today's dollars, $250,000 equals approximately $1,250,000. The average CEO pay of a Fortune 500 company today exceeds $10,000,000. If an average production worker's pay had increased proportionately to CEO pay since this book was written, she would earn nearly $170,000 a year. Instead, she earned $27,460 in 2004.

---

* I was still making $36,000.

PROMISES

Keep them. If asked when you can deliver something, ask for time to think. Build in a margin of safety. Name a date. Then deliver it earlier than you promised.

The world is divided into two classes of people: the few people who make good on their promises (even if they don't promise as much), and the many who don't. Get in column A and stay there. You'll be very valuable wherever you are.

You might suppose that the higher you go in the ranks of business executives, the more word-keepers you find. My experience doesn't substantiate this. I've been welshed on by a big bank president, the number two man of a major finance company and various investment banking house partners. I only know four people who I'm sure won't break their word at any price.★

★ You remember the old story about the philosopher who asked a beautiful socialite at a cocktail party if she would sleep with him for $5 million. She said she would. He asked, "How about $5?" She was outraged. "What do you think I am—a whore?" "We've already established that," said the philosopher, "now I'm trying to establish your price."

PROMOTION, FROM WITHIN

Most managements complain about the lack of able people and go outside to fill key positions. Nonsense. Nobody inside an organization ever looked ready to move into a bigger job.

I use the rule of 50 per cent. Try to find somebody inside the company with a record of success (in any area) and with an appetite for the job. If he looks like 50 per cent of what you need, give him the job. In six months he'll have grown the other 50 per cent and everybody will be satisfied.

How to do it wrong: go outside and get some expensive guy* who looks like 110 per cent of what you want and a year later, after having raised salaries all around him, you'll still be teaching him the business. The people around him will be frustrated and ineffective.

One of the keys is to pick someone within the company who has a well-deserved reputation as a winner. Not someone who looks to you like a *potential* winner but doesn't happen to be fitting in very well where he is.

The organization will rally around an accepted winner, even when he's temporarily over his head, because in their eyes he deserves the chance. The phony who conned you into giving him the job will go down for the third time and pull down everybody else he can reach.

* Like Bunky Knudsen or Bo Polk.

PUBLIC ACCOUNTANTS AND THE AUDIT COMMITTEE

With the controller's full understanding and agreement, the first time the chief executive meets with his outside auditing team (including the partner in charge) he should say something like this: "We want our accounts to be honest and to give a fair picture of our performance. No matter how bad. Here's a letter from me asking you to report promptly to the audit committee of the board any attempt on my part or anyone else's to influence you otherwise." Then he should ask the auditors to be forthright in their audit report. Too often, problems in an early stage may be only hinted at.

Public accounting firms are expensive. Partners are billed around seventy-five dollars an hour, senior associates around fifty dollars an hour, junior associates around thirty-five dollars an hour. Your audit bill will be lower if you encourage the controller to get as much of the routine work done in house before those big meters start ticking.

Ad agencies love to spend your money on market research, and lawyers on legal research. CPA firms all have systems departments and it doesn't take much to start them doing systems work. With all three groups it is well to set up some kind of general alarm that goes off before you accidentally discover they've spent a lot of your money doing work you don't want done.

The audit committee should be two or three independent outside directors. Four is a bull session, one's not enough.

They should meet with the outside auditors after the annual audit report comes out, but at least a week before the board of directors meeting to which they will report.

They invite members of management (including the chief executive) at their pleasure into and out of the meeting. Alone with the auditors, they can and should ask questions that would be embarrassing at other times during the year: "Has anyone pressed you to do anything you're reluctant to do?" "Is there any subject or incident that for any reason you didn't include or didn't give proper weight to in the audit report that you'd like to discuss orally now?"

When the audit committee is satisfied that all material questions have been asked, and honest answers given (whether favorable or unfavorable), they are ready to report to the board of directors.

PURCHASING DEPARTMENT

Yes, fire the whole purchasing department.★

They cost ten dollars in zeal for every dollar they save through purchasing acumen.

And that doesn't count the massive unrecorded disasters they cause. Let's say somebody has persuaded a young Edison or Steinmetz to go to work for General Conglobulation, Inc. By the time he's found out that there's no way to get that $900 desk calculator through the purchasing department he's lost all respect for General Conglobulation ("They'd hire Einstein and then turn down his requisition for a blackboard").

So let's be sensible. Fire the whole purchasing department. The company will benefit from having each department dealing in the free market outside instead of being victimized by internal socialism.† And don't underestimate the morale value of letting your people "waste" some money. If you must, have a one-man "buying department" (*see* Personnel [People vs.] for the parallel idea of a one-girl people department) for those who want help in the purchasing area and ask for it.

★ Obviously I was thinking about service businesses. In manufacturing, purchasing should be a function of engineering and production. If some one elsewhere in the company needs a stopwatch, he should be free to call the purchasing department or buy it direct if purchasing is too ridden with forms and procedures.

† I'm told that the federal government, with all their joint-use purchasing economies, really pays 20 per cent more for a pencil than you do at the five-and-ten.

PUTTING ON WEIGHT

A sure sign of frustration is putting on weight. Watch for it on the people who work for you. Remove the cause and the weight will come back off.

Editor's Note: According to the U.S. Department of Health and Human Services, the weight of the average American increased by 24 pounds from 1960 to 2002.

R RACISM

Let's face it. The vast majority of corporations are still operating with dice loaded against Jews, black people, and women of all races and creeds.

Well, it must be clear by now to everybody in touch with reality that it's time to unload the dice. This has to start with a conviction in the chief executive officer. But if he wants more than a scurry by each division to find a company black,★ he better follow up his bulletin as far down the line as he can and for as long as he is chief executive. Stamping out racism will be a process, not an act, and the chief resistance will be in the personnel office. It is results, not explanations, that count, as in other business action, and you can waste a lot of time just talking.

★ Things are looking up. You don't hear about the company "Nigger" much any more, and the company "Kike" is now the company Jew. Women are still bottom-of-the-heap: "Don't give her a raise; she's making a lot *for a woman.*"

REORGANIZING

Should be undergone about as often as major surgery. And should be as well planned and as swiftly executed.

*I was to learn later in life that we tend to meet any new situation by reorganizing; and a wonderful method it can be for creating the illusion of progress while producing confusion, inefficiency, and demoralization.**

★ From Petronius Arbiter (circa A.D. 60).

RETIREMENT, MANDATORY

A sound idea for now. But it can be carried too far. About ten years ago, American Express put through automatic across-the-board retirement at age sixty-five. Their travel competitors threw their caps in the air. Seems that certain tour guides, like '45, '59, and '61 wines from the great vineyards of Bordeaux, get better with age. So I'd exempt specialists who have no other people reporting to them.

Early retirement is also sound, to take care of people who, like '51 and '54 vintages, didn't work out.

More important than either is to retire the chief executive every five or six years (*see* Wearing Out Your Welcome).

S SALARY REVIEW: ANNUAL ENCOUNTER GROUP

Once a year the chief executive officer should review all the salaries of the people reporting to him for relative fairness (not performance). Then he calls in all those people and together they review the salaries of all the people reporting to them in the same light. It's an uncomfortable meeting, but it's only once a year. And by doing it all out in the open you compensate for the fact that some bosses are better salesmen for their people than others.

If this is done right, you can honestly say to people reporting to you who bug you about salary in between annual reviews: "Look, everybody is always either overpaid or underpaid. Let *me* worry about you. If *you* worry about you, you'll be less effective and earn less than you should. Concentrate on your job and look up after every salary review to see if you are being fairly treated."

SALESMEN

1. Twenty per cent of any given group of salesmen will always produce 80 per cent of the sales.
2. A good incentive-compensation scale for salesmen slides up: 5 per cent on the first $100,000 sales; 7½ per cent on the second $100,000, and so forth. And don't modify it if some hot salesman brings down the chandeliers and earns a fortune. That's what you wanted, dummy. The word will go through the sales grapevine and the salesmen's wives' grapevine and you won't believe the results.
3. Top salesmen (all salesmen if you can work it) should be given stock options and encouraged to think like owners.
4. A good way to kill a top salesmen is to promote him to assistant sales manager.★ A manager is one breed, a salesman is another. Most good salesmen thrive in the field, wither at headquarters. "There I was alone," a true salesman once said, "with nothing but my golden voice."

★ A viable theory is the Peter Principle: "In a hierarchy, every employee tends to rise to his level of incompetence (the cream rises until it sours)." Peter's corollary: "In time every post tends to be occupied by an employee who is incompetent to carry out its duties." From *The Peter Principle* by Peter and Hull. New York: Morrow; 1969.

SECRECY: A CHILD'S GARDEN OF DISEASES

Secrecy is totally bad. It defeats the crusade for justice, which doesn't flourish in the dark.

Did you ever ask yourself why there's a private payroll? Or why all wages and salaries aren't posted on the bulletin board? According to the lore of the free-enterprise system money is really a scorecard. So why aren't the scores posted?★

Of course the company would have a revulsion (or a revolution) if everybody had to look squarely at a list showing the salaries of the president and his nephew, who are paid four times what they're worth, and the salaries of Izzy, Derek, and Susie, who are making a third of what they're worth.

In the case of most marketing or new product planning, secrecy is sinister. It defeats your loyal opposition and protects you from your best friends when you need them most. Secrecy implies either:

1. *What I'm doing is so horrible I don't dare tell you.*

or

2. *I don't trust you (any more).*

★ I'm not suggesting that you should post salaries. For one thing, it would over-emphasize the importance of money. But you shouldn't tolerate a situation in which you're *ashamed* to post them. Like you are.

SECRETARY, FREEDOM FROM A

For years I had the standard executive equipment—a secretary. Most of them very good. Then I used the Man from Mars approach. Then I didn't have a secretary. Here's my analysis:

TELEPHONE

Before	*After*
Jane took all my calls and made all my calls (it really has to be all one or all the other). Two of the many games we played: "How long shall I let it ring before I decide she's not there?" "Shall I interrupt his meeting with this call?" (How many meetings, finally at the nitty-gritty, are interrupted by your secretary asking if you want to take a call, and you never seem to get back on the track whether you take the call or not?)	The telephone operators took all my calls until eleven in the morning saying, "May I have Mr. Townsend call you back?" Then at eleven, they'd send all the call messages in, start putting incoming calls through, and I would do the dialing myself. Result: Nobody mad. (Note, no offense because when she offers to have me call back, she hasn't asked who you are.) My calls were concentrated in a forty-five-minute period. I'm on the phone first (one-up). Same thing from lunch until four o'clock, when the afternoon call messages were sent in, and incoming calls were put through again.

Before	*After*
APPOINTMENTS	
I'd come back from a one-day trip or even a long lunch to find my calendar cluttered with appointments with my own people.	Since there was no one to make an appointment with, people would stick their heads in. If I wasn't there, they'd come back later, or change their minds. Interruptions? A few. But that's what I'm there for.
MAIL	
Jane would read it first. What with interruptions it was generally the next morning before I got the replies back for signature.	Had two sets of note pads. One with just my name. The other, for strangers who wrote to the office, had my name, title, address, phone number. Handwritten replies.
	Advantages: Impressed the recipients. No files. Can be done on trips, weekends, early morning, evening. Lots faster. The infrequent letter that needed typing was done by staff services. If I wanted a Xerox of my note, I'd write "copy" in the corner.

| *Before* | *After* |

FILES

Jane filed copies of everything. Just to be sure. Spent a lot of time at the Xerox machine or in transit. Finally had to have more space for her third four-drawer file cabinet.

Emptied all three file cabinets. What I kept filled half the file drawer in my desk. When that filled up, I'd weed it back to half. If you ever get a serious antitrust action, the thing that will hang you (even if you're innocent) will be Jane's files.

TRIPS

One of my close associates had a great secretary. Whenever he called in from out of town to get or leave messages, she was "away from her desk." And when he came back, she would have all the mail and memos and appointments spread out so he couldn't find his desk for two days.

When I called in the telephone operators had my messages. The mailroom also had a rubber stamp: "I'm away. Please handle this in your own style and don't tell me what you did. Thanks. R.C.T." They'd open the mail, stamp it, route it appropriately. When I got back—clean desk.

Morning coffee, in-box, out-box, Xeroxing, and other matters were handled by staff services. An important thing I learned was that my secretary had been acting like an assistant-to. Helping me where I didn't want and couldn't be helped. Playing favorites with my associates. I got much closer to the people who reported to me when I didn't have a buffer state outside my office.

Working without a secretary depends on a good staff-services operation (*see* Staff Services [Steno Pool]). And making friends with the telephone operators, which is a breeze when they find out you're going to can your secretary. Telephone operators and executive secretaries are natural enemies.

Build a good staff-services setup and then try to persuade your executives to give it a good fair try for a month every time somebody's secretary quits, or for however long she's sick or having a baby or on vacation. In my case, unloading a secretary worked out like finding an extra four hours a day.

SMALL COMPANIES

... trying to make the transition to big publicly owned companies tend to make the same mistake.

They look at General Motors and see finance committees, executive committees, planning departments, advertising departments, marketing departments, personnel departments, management development departments, and public relations departments, and they say, "Aha, so that's how they do it!" And a year later they're out of business. If Alfred Sloan had started with all that crap there wouldn't be a General Motors to look at.

If you're a small or medium-size business trying to make the grade, you're going to have to take on a few of the burdens of the publicly owned companies. But only a few. And for that reason carefully examine every new expense and activity to see whether it's a necessity or an ornament.

If *your* problem, like that of General Motors, is to keep your share of the market below 55 per cent and your operating profit margin below 20 per cent, then go and do likewise. But I'm afraid you'll be like the poor old lady who thought all she had to do to become an opera singer was to drink lots of heavy cream—you'll be confusing fat with muscle.

Editor's Note: In fact, GM's market share has never exceeded 50 percent. It was approximately 45 percent at the time this was written, and had declined to 25 percent by late 2006. The company is cash-negative at this writing, and it posted a $1.1 billion loss in just one quarter in 2006.

STAFF SERVICES (STENO POOL)*

You can't call it steno pool. It brings to mind the dregs of the office. My steno pool I call staff services. And there must be a better name. It serves the brightest executives, including the chief executive officer, because they don't have secretaries.

The staff-services office is luxuriously furnished and the girls are recruited from the ranks of the best secretaries in the area. And paid top salaries.

One of them brings you your coffee, empties your out-basket, does your Xeroxing, brings your mail, poses as your secretary (to a caller who won't believe you don't have a secretary), takes dictation in your office or from your dictaphone belts.

Since there are, say, ten of them for twenty executives, your secretary is never sick. Since the girls are paid more than the secretaries of executives who insist on owning a girl, and since the day goes faster if you're busy (and what secretary for one man is constantly busy?), their morale is high and the pressure is from girls trying to get *into* the group, not out of it.

Please get it through your head. You're not trying to save money. That was the steno-pool idea. You're trying to improve the secretarial services without spending any more money and without having a lot of half-occupied women wandering around looking for trouble.

Editor's Note: The rather egregious and liberal use of the word "girl" in this entry was eliminated in the next edition.

---

* *See also* Telephone Operators.

STOCKHOLDERS

As is well known, the big corporation's priorities are:

1. *Care and feeding of the chief executive, his entourage, and the board of directors (mostly his friends, put there by him to ensure the tranquility of his reign).*
2. *Management.*
3. *Employees.*
4. *Customers.*
5. *(Way down the line) Stockholders.*

Only very rarely is the stockholder mentioned in a company. I suggest a different set of priorities:

1. *Stockholders. Turn the management and as many employees as possible into stockholders—and with enough stock so they think of themselves as owners.**
2. *This makes the customer important.*
3. *Management and employees are taken care of by their success as stockholders as well as by a healthier company that can afford to pay top salaries.*
4. *In my Utopian corporation, directors are last priority. They are paid nothing, attend meetings because they are stockholders, get monthly figures, meet quarterly for an all-day report on the state and trend of the business, and are concerned solely with putting out dividends and chief executives.*

---

* Professional managers are cautious because they have to prove they're right; owner-managed companies take more chances and their timing is better because it's their money on the line and they have the right to try something they can't prove.

STOCK OPTIONS AND DEMOCRACY

The traditional approach is that options are for the top $\frac{1}{10}$ of 1 per cent—for one out of a thousand workers.

Misguided. More of your people must be owners. Your lawyers and investment bankers will try to talk you out of this sensible impulse, but the deeper you can spread ownership the better.

One of the reasons Sears Roebuck is an exception to the fat lethargy rule of big, mature, successful companies is that 200,000, or almost 60 per cent, of their people own 35,000,000 shares, or 22 per cent of the company, through the "Employees' Profit-Sharing Fund." This holding is worth more than $2 billion: over $10,000 per participant.

T TAX ADVICE

You ask your law firm to recommend a tax man from among their partners, and you ask your public accounting firm to do the same. You talk to the two men and try to get them interested in your business. Then, as in the choice of a lawyer, you pick the one who will give you his home phone and who will listen to your problem, ask questions, and then call you back within twenty-four hours with his opinion.

Big-company-style tax men are murder. They judge themselves by how many pros and cons they can dream up, and how many alternate methods might be "worth investigating." You need a man who will say, "If I were you and had to make a decision and then get back to minding the store, I'd do this."

TEAMS, TWO-MAN—
GOOD AND BAD

I've long held the opinion that a two-man chief executive is the answer. Look at the poor President of the United States, and what he tries to do in a given day or week. No wonder our country has been in a leadership crisis for twenty-five years.

But it isn't easy.

The two men have to complement each other, and above all trust each other implicitly. They both have to have a sense of humor and they have to enjoy working together. Each must respect the other's fundamental instincts, not just in talk but in action. If you're about to do something that your partner might be nervous about, you ask if he has a conviction against it. The do-you-have-a-conviction game is about the only way to keep from driving each other up the wall.

The worst two-man team I ever saw tried to act like the Bobbsey twins even though 3,000 miles normally separated them. They tried to keep each other totally informed at all times *in advance.* I suppose the idea was that then they'd share the responsibility for mistakes. But in addition to being time-consuming, this method *reduces* accountability. "Oh well, Bill knew about it in advance and went along with the idea." Instead of, "Holy mackerel, I'm out here all by myself, I better find a way to make this work, or kill it before it gets out of control."

The best two-man team I ever saw started with the philosophy: Neither of us is very good, but our weaknesses (and strengths) may be compensating. Like yang and yin, man and wife. We expect to make a lot of mistakes, but we hope to have the courage to correct them no matter how silly we look in the process. If we do our best, split up the chores, check in advance on strategic matters, and keep each other informed after the fact on the daily disasters, we'll have fun.

Sample telephone conversations:

1. *"If you don't have a conviction, I'm going to do this about that . . ."*
2. *"Unless you object, I'm going to take on this [task, opportunity, problem, obstacle]. I'll let you know how I did."* That means I'll call you in a week or six months or whenever it's over. It doesn't mean I'll keep you posted on each day's triumph or tribulation.
3. *"This needs doing. Will you do it? I'm no good at it."*
4. *"Do you know about . . . ?" "Yes, I'm going to take care of it when the time is right."* Or, *"Good grief, I forgot all about it. I'll do it right now. Thanks."*
5. *"You remember I told you I'd take care of . . . Well, this is what I finally did. This is what I should have done. This is what it cost the company. How's that for wasting money?"*
6. In the matter of strategic (expensive-to-correct) decisions: *"I've thought through the XYZ matter. There are three ways to go: the first looks like this; the second looks like this; and the third looks like this. I've got no real conviction but I'm inclined to [or I feel strongly that we should] go the second route."*

In this instance and at this point it is strongly advisable for the speaker to sit back and listen. Often he'll hear: *"It's a tough choice, do whatever you think is right,"* or, *"Sounds right to me."* Occasionally, a good listener will hear: *"You fathead! What's the matter with the fourth way?"* I've saved a lot of money listening for that sound, no matter how I cringed at the time.

I've known three-man chief executive teams that worked where two were in one location and one in another. But not very well and not for long.

TELEPHONE OPERATORS

If I ever design a head office, executive row will look like the cubicles of a Trappist monastery, and the telephone-switchboard area will look like a Turkish harem. Money spent on offices for the management is largely wasted. If they are any good it will be apparent to anyone after a few minutes no matter how plain or fancy their office is.

On the other hand, how would you like to try doing the telephone operator's job for a day? Remember, you're the company's first contact with the outside world—you've got to be alert and bright and helpful and quick. You've got to know where everybody is all the time. I'd spend money to make the switchboard girls comfortable. The best operators in the area would be lined up for the job.

THANKS

A really neglected form of compensation.

TIME: THREE THOUGHTS ON IT

Small companies should be fun. The key people frequently work six days and all hours and get very expert. That's a 20 per cent edge over the nine-to-five five-days-a-week big-business operation.

New people need time to earn their place on a team. New systems need time to shake down. Lots of people are quick with the torpedoes on new people and new systems. Give them time.

Some meetings should be long and leisurely. Some should be mercifully brief. A good way to handle the latter is to hold the meeting with everybody standing up. The meetees won't believe you at first. Then they get very uncomfortable and can hardly wait to get the meeting over with. If you have more than one comfortable chair for office visitors, move to a smaller office.

TITLES ARE HANDY TOOLS★

There is a trade-off here. In one way, titles are a form of psychic compensation, and if too many titles are distributed, the currency is depreciated. But a title is also a tool. If our salesman is a vice-president and yours is a sales rep, and both are in a waiting room, guess who gets in first and gets the most attention.

If you find you can't get applicants for menial jobs, maybe your titles are obsolete. Nobody today can tell his girl he's a clerk or a busboy. One airline improved a bad situation by changing "ramp service clerk" to "ramp service engineer." A restaurant cured a chronic busboy shortage by changing the title to "logistics engineer."

★ *See* Chairman of the Executive Committee for further thoughts on titles.

TOO MUCH VS. TOO LITTLE

Too little is almost always better than too much.

Space: Too much brings out the worst in empire builders. They'll fill up the excess so fast you'll wind up with too little again. Too little makes you creative in your use of people. Too much puts the company emphasis on office grandeur, not on service and performance.★

People: One person with only half a job can wander around and do real damage in his or her spare time. The best organizations are sufficiently understaffed so that if somebody does something that overlaps or invades your area of responsibility, your second reaction is: "Great! If you've got time to do that, *you* do it from now on." This feeling comes right after the first flash of territorial hostility. Organizations that have time to get into jurisdictional disputes are almost always overstaffed.

Money: A tight budget brings out the best creative instincts in man. Give him unlimited funds and he won't come up with the best way to a result. Man is a complicating animal. He only simplifies under pressure. Put him under some financial pressure. He'll scream in anguish. Then he'll come up with a plan which, to his own private amazement, is not only less expensive, but also faster and better than his original proposal, which you sent back.

★ At Avis I resisted demands for more space at headquarters. While we grew from $30 million to $75 million, we stayed in 30,000 square feet. "Double-decker desks" was a common joke. When the demands became too insistent, I let a couple of units move into neighboring buildings. But only units with a profit center of their own. At least there you have the performance yardstick of profit. But let a service function like accounting move out, and if separation doesn't work, they may take out their frustration in empire building before you realize what's happening.

TRAINING

The only way I know to get somebody trained is on the job. The first time I learned this was by accident. I'd laboriously recruited an assistant (note: not an assistant-to). By the time I'd offered the job and he'd accepted I was pretty sure I had a good man. But the earliest he could come to work was the day I left for vacation. Turmoil! Should I go? For the wrong reasons I went.

Thrown in the deep end, he learned some plain and fancy swimming while I was away. And he developed some valuable relationships in those three weeks that might never have developed if I'd been there. He got in the habit of growing and has never stopped.

If you have more than one possible successor, *never* anoint a favorite. You'll stop the healthy competition for your job and paint a bull's-eye on your heir's shirt-front. I did it once, and the organization tore him to shreds. Better to keep an open-minded show-me attitude toward all contenders.

Every time I left the office for more than a week, I'd write the following memo:

To: *People who report to me*
Date: *Today*
cc: *Mailroom*
Owner
Telephone Operators

I've gone away. Until I get back Henry is chief executive officer. Please don't hold up decisions. Anything you do in my absence will have my complete support when I return. R.C.T.

Two things about this. Rotate the acting successor if you can. Otherwise you've named your heir. And don't say where you've gone or when you'll be back.

Remember, you really want them to make some important decisions and some mistakes (*see* Mistakes). That's how they grow.

U UNDERPAID

Some good people become badly underpaid. If you're in this spot, but like your work, cheer up; all is not lost.

Resign. Go to the personnel department. Fill in the forms. Apply for your old position. Under "salary objective" put down what you should be paid.

If your diagnosis is correct, you'll be far and away the best-qualified applicant for your old job and cheap at the new price. When I bullied a griping friend into doing this, he ended up with a 30 per cent pay raise, in a company that didn't believe in paying people.

If they don't rehire you because of "regulations," it's time you left the company anyway, because they've got the tail on the front of the dog.

V VACATION POLICY: GO WHEN YOU PLEASE

Just like office hours, vacations for people who make more than $150 a week should be left up to each individual. No responsible people will abuse the freedom. Your worst job will be running your best people out of town when they need some play time.

Editor's Note: $150 per week equaled $755 in today's dollars, or approximately $40,000 annual salary.

W WASHINGTON, D.C., RELATIONS WITH

Businessmen often underestimate the number of able, conscientious, and zealous people working for government in Washington—and Albany, Springfield, and Sacramento. They're usually overworked and underpaid. And motivated primarily by pride and faith in what they're doing. Try treating them that way.

Don't use a prestigious Washington law firm to represent you in ordinary★ government relations. All the ready-made defenses click into place when Clark Clifford's boys call up.

But when your lawyer from Terre Haute telephones, it's an event. It's different. They have no idea who he is, and no way of making sure. He can walk in and say "You're my government . . . help me." And they will. And love him for asking. It's a refreshing change for them from the hot-shot New York and Washington lawyers who have all the answers and are telling . . . not asking.

Editor's Note: Townsend refers to three Washington insiders in this entry. Clark McAdams Clifford (1906–1998) was a powerful attorney who served Presidents Truman, Kennedy, Johnson, and Carter. "Tommy the Cork" is Thomas Corcoran, considered by some to be the first modern lobbyist. Lloyd Cutler was White House Counsel in the Carter and Clinton administrations.

★ In a major emergency, however, there is no substitute for Tommy the Cork, Lloyd Cutler, or someone of that ilk.

WEARING OUT YOUR WELCOME

Nobody should be chief executive officer of anything for more than five or six years. By then he's stale, bored, and utterly dependent on his own clichés—though they may have been revolutionary ideas when he first brought them to the office.

Also, decisions aren't based on consensus, but on one man's view of what's best for the organization. And that means even the best decisions make some people unhappy. After five or six years a good chief will have absorbed all the hostility he can take, and his decisions will be reflecting a desire to avoid pain rather than to do what's right.

In 1940, when Sewell Avery had completed eight years as chief executive of Montgomery Ward, that company's common stock was valued in the stock market at $200 million compared to $500 million for competitor Sears Roebuck. Avery stayed fourteen more years and a race became no contest. In mid-1967, before Montgomery Ward disappeared from the stock market by merger, its common stock was valued at $400 million—a double in twenty-seven years. Sears Roebuck in mid-1967 was worth $9 billion—18 times as much as in 1940.

Lesson for stockholders and directors: If the chief executive doesn't retire gracefully after five or six years—throw the rascal out.

APPENDIX: RATE YOUR BOSS AS A LEADER

Score each characteristic from 0 to 10

He is

1. ... *available. If I have a problem I can't solve, he is there. But he is forceful in making me do my level best to bring in solutions, not problems.* _____
2. ... *inclusive. Quick to let me in on information or people who might be useful to me or stimulating or of long-term professional interest.* _____
3. ... *humorous. Has a full measure of the Comic Spirit in his make-up. Laughs even harder when the joke's on him.* _____
4. ... *fair. And concerned about me and how I'm doing. Gives credit where credit is due, but holds me to my promise.* _____
5. ... *decisive. Determined to get at those little unimportant (how they are decided) decisions which can tie up organizations for days.* _____
6. ... *humble. Admits his own mistakes openly— learns from them and expects his people to do the same.* _____
7. ... *objective. Knows the apparently important (like a visiting director) from the truly important (a meeting of his own people) and goes where he is needed.* _____

8. . . . tough. Won't let top management or important
    outsiders waste his time or his people's time. Is more
    jealous of his people's time than he is of his own.   _____

9. . . . effective. Teaches me to bring him my mistakes
    with what I've learned (if anything) and done about
    them (if anything). Teaches me not to interrupt him
    with possible good news on which no action is needed.   _____

10. . . . patient. Knows when to bite the bullet until I
    solve my own problem.   _____

                                        Total★   _____

★ This is your boss's rating as a leader on a scale of 0 to 100. If it's below 50 look
for another job.

FURTHER "UP THE ORGANIZATION"

ENCOURAGE TREASON. Whenever anyone says he's been offered a job by another company, don't get possessive. Encourage him to review seriously what he isn't getting out of his present job (and what he is) and see if he can better himself enough to warrant a change.

If he decides to stay, he'll buckle down and work more effectively than ever. The result is worth the week or so of inattention. And your objectivity and friendliness will help him come to a better decision sooner.

You can wince, but if you're genuinely interested in your people, how can you do anything but rejoice if they get an offer you can't match?

DISTRUST YOUR INSTINCTS. With whom would you *least* like to have a nice long shoptalk?

Right. The fellow who's working on about your level over in that other division; the one who keeps getting in your hair.

So go see him. Right now. It'll be the best thing you do today.

Instincts were designed to help us survive the climb from the primordial slime, not to guide us through the day in a modern bureaucracy.

Ask yourself two questions every morning:

1. Who do I least want to see?
2. What do I least want to do?

Chances are they'll be your top priority for that day.

RUBBER CHICKEN. You're sitting in the middle of the Waldorf-Astoria grand ballroom. It's ten p.m. and the Great Man is drawing to a close with an appeal that we all pull together.

Not bloody likely.

For four and a half hours, you've had more elbows stuck into you than a professional hockey player in a full season. You've been fed two weak drinks, four helpings of inane conversation (two on either side) and a year's supply of carbohydrates (you ate two rolls and the baked Alaska out of desperation). It'll take you an hour to get home. You feel like you're coming down with a cold. And now you're looking around at a room full of idiots like yourself who are looking around, wondering how in hell they got roped into this thing again.

Can we abandon these barbaric bores?

A tempting thought; but, instead, let's make them more enjoyable and productive.

If you were a visitor from another planet, had never been to one of these affairs and were asked to make it reasonably useful, what would you do?

Abolish the dais.

Label prominent people (normally on the dais) with puce (for prominent) tags and place one at each table.

Schedule the speech at seven p.m. sharp, *before dinner.*

At intervals, during dinner introduce puce tags and conduct all the necessary ritual, if any. Mostly, however, there should be a discussion of the speech at each table, hopefully enlivened by the presence of a seminal mind.

After dinner, a five-minute break for the departure of those who know by now that this speaker isn't going to challenge or inform them.

Question-and-answer period. Blunt. Real questions. At some point, the chairman should tell everybody that they can go home unless they want to participate in the further grilling of the speaker until he calls it quits.

The times of the speech and the Q.-and-A. session should be indicated on the invitation—and abided by. Otherwise, a lot of late arrivals will wind up with just ritual and rubber chicken.

THE BUSINESS LUNCH. People seem to be afraid to meet one another except over a meal. The result is that two busy executives who need to see each other tomorrow can't get together for the next three weeks.

Solution: 1. Don't make lunch dates. 2. When you want to see someone, call and ask if you can go over now or later today or tomorrow morning. Invite people who want to see you to do likewise.

And think of all you can accomplish between twelve and two, while your friends buck traffic and stretch their weight belts.

FIRST PRIZE: Two weeks in Philadelphia. If you become an outstanding performer, your corporate reward may be a ticket to oblivion. Not intentionally. It's just because top managements, in between golf games, outside board meetings and charity drives, spend their time assigning their best people to problems instead of to opportunities. If you do a spectacular job with *Time,* therefore, you may be asked to save *Life.* But before you accept, satisfy yourself that the job you're being offered is (A) doable and (B) worth doing.

Lots of stars have accepted mission-impossibles and wound up whistling, "Who knows where the time goes?" in the company cemetery.

Top managements, be warned: After Hercules cleaned out the stables, he slew Augeas for asking him to do it.

ORGANIZATION CHARTS AND RECTAN-GULAR PEOPLE. Don't print and circulate organization charts. They mislead you and everybody else into wasting time conning one another. Anyway, you probably spend a major fraction of your time dealing directly with people who aren't really above or below you on the chart. Don't let yourself be conned into thinking you relate only up or down and sideways to peers. If people are off to one side but *below* you on the chart, you may be tempted to ignore them, summon them to your office or at least assume they'll do whatever you want. In your own self-interest, to avoid their attack, or to enlist their required support in advance, you should go to *them* at *their* convenience to explain and persuade.

The head of the mail room or the chief telephone operator may hold your destiny someday. Figure out who's important to your effectiveness and then *treat him (or her) that way.*

It wouldn't hurt to assume, in short, that every man—and woman—is a human being, not a rectangle.

THE SURE-FIRE TOWNSEND INNOVATION TEST. If you come up with a new idea for your department or division, you can get an almost infallible early reading on it.

1. If everybody gives it something between active indifference and hot opposition, the idea is valid. Also, the importance of the idea will be directly proportional to the amount of passionate opposition it stirs up.
2. If everybody drops dead from enthusiasm for your idea, it's certainly minor and probably wrong. You may be telling them what they want to hear upstairs. And hot new ideas never come from up there.

CAMPUS RECRUITING. Send the people who can't go.

To convert a corporate liability into an asset overnight, fire the recruiters and put together a group of the most active, enthusiastic and successful people at work in your company, at all levels. Make them the campus recruiters. Their job: to be honest, not to sell or persuade.

The young prospects will spot the difference. Your man, who is on top of a job that he believes in, will be worth 40 personnel-department zombies who improvise answers and deal in images.

Your part-time recruiters will plead that they're too busy to take on this chore, but it's worth it to persuade them. They'll come back freshened up by their trip behind the Beard Curtain. Who knows, they may pick up an idea.

When their recruiting starts to pay off, make them into an *ad hoc* committee on how to turn the graduates loose on real jobs—to find out which ones weren't turned into sullen slaves by 20 years of classroom dictatorship.

By the way, fire the training department. These baby sitters in the corporate kindergartens can turn any job into busy seatwork.

MONEY AT THE TOP. The best boss to work for—if you can find him—is one who's made enough keeping money (over $1,000,000 after taxes) by his own efforts so that he can walk out the door if he gets pushed too hard from upstairs in a direction he knows is wrong. He runs his outfit like he owns it.

Too much *inherited* keeping money (over $5,000,000) is a birth defect. It produces high and visible insecurity. When concentrated in outrageous amounts, it tempts Daddy to buy control of U.S. Environment Corporation for Sonny to play with. That's not all bad, because it makes a bleeding genius out of whoever follows Sonny. But, in a way, it's unfair. Edgar Bronfman, for example, may be a great chief executive at Seagrams. Nobody'll ever find out.

A family megafortune guarantees a chief executive two deadly plagues for life:

1. A cloud of charm boys will always distort his view of reality and give him a chronic case of corporate pinkeye.
2. The real and total resentment of the poor slobs doing the work will make them withhold the early warnings he needs to get from the front.

Moral: If your company gets bought for Sonny—hang in there. If Sonny is lucky, he'll be out on his ass and some genius—why not you?—will be sitting in his office in no time at all.

HOT AIR FROM COLD SALESMEN. Pity the poor salesman. He's out there with nothing but his talent and your product and he has to come back to write a sales report. If he hasn't made it, he has to say why. That's when the worst salesmen become the best experts on product redesign.

They've got plenty of ideas to draw on. No salesman ever makes the circuit without hearing: "We would buy your product if it were:

(A)   built sideways, or
(B)   turned over, or
(C)   painted blue, or
(D)   if it included this one simple added feature." (All this is rarely true but it's easier for a buyer to say than no.)

So when the bullshit salesman makes his no-sales report, he must do one of two things: (A) admit, in effect, that he's lousy, or (B) offer excuses: "The whole trouble is product design. . . ."

As product redesigners, marketing vice-presidents are twice as dangerous as salesmen, which is the second reason you shouldn't have any (for the first, *see* Marketing). They talk the marketing language of the Harvard Business School, a peculiar jargon full of practical sounding "unit margins" and "bottom-line pay-offs." It makes hot air sound like hard sense. Worse yet, marketeers love to have lunch with the kind of media supermarketeers whose by-lines appear over fatuous forecasts in industrial trade journals and newsletters. Any one of these natural gassers can fill your marketing v.p. with enough random farts to blow the whole Common Market apart, let alone your pitiful little company.

THE SABOTAGE OF FREE ENTERPRISE. If you're going to function effectively in our organizational society, it's important that you have a healthy contempt for our major institutions, public and private—and especially for their leaders. These clowns are not entitled to the respect they get as the vestal virgins of our society.

It's not clear to me exactly when "free enterprise" became a joke. Was it after the Civil War, when big business, big government and the Supreme Court formed an unholy alliance to exploit the American farmer and laborer? Or was it later, when big labor got a partnership? Or when big military elbowed up to the trough? Or when big education cut itself in on the deal?

Whenever it was, the heart of the conspiracy today against the American consumer is the New York–Washington axis, and our real adversaries are big lawyers, top Government officials and high officers of big corporations.

When the American system falls, it won't be Communists who bring it down. We aren't in any danger of being destroyed from the outside; we've perfected do-it-yourself methods.

Our blowup will come when the American housewife discovers that Clark Clifford arranged for her to pay half of the punitive-damage fines General Electric got socked with for conspiring to defraud the American housewife. He persuaded the IRS to accept the fines as tax deductions. This is the moral equivalent of letting the meat packers deduct as an ordinary business expense the cost of the ingredient they use to make putrescent meat look healthy, so they can still sell it to you.

It's no wonder you can't get senior partners of major law firms to work weekends. I sympathize with them. If I were doing to America what they're doing to it from ten to six Monday through Friday, I'd have to get stoned on Saturday and Sunday, too.

PROTECTING THE GUILTY. A typical company agrees to indemnify its officers and directors. That is, if I'm sued and convicted as an officer of a drug company for knowingly letting a harmful drug murder or deform a few thousand people, my company will pay the $2500 fine and my legal expenses and deduct them from income (for tax purposes) as ordinary business expense. (Judging by the Allison case, where a known defective airplane engine caused the death of 38 people, corporate manslaughter costs about $200 a head.)

So the Government subsidizes murder.

All officers and directors should pay their own fines and legal expenses, and the amounts paid should be reported in proxy statements along with salaries (now reported) and expense accounts (not now reported).

You may have noted that this modest proposal does not come to grips with the main problem—the double standard by which the law protects a corporate agent from the responsibilities normally weighed against a private citizen. If I shoot my neighbor, chances are I'll be severely punished for my crime. But if, in my job, I'm convicted of withholding information about a dangerous product that leads to the death of thousands of my neighbors, the most I'll get is a civil suit that amounts to a slap on the wrist.

This is because our brightest lawyers have been working for years to preserve the myth (which their antecedents created) that criminal law doesn't apply to what I do as a *corporate executive;* that's covered by the civil code. (In Britain, corporate signatures end in "Ltd." That means "limited liability." The Latins are more poetic and descriptive: They use "S.A."—*Sociedad Anónima,* or Society of the Nameless. It all adds up to the same thing: When the cops come, there's nobody home.)

This legal anomaly has led to all sorts of aberrant corporate behavior.

Insurance companies, for example, don't disclose auto-accident statistics by make of vehicle, which would tend to warn their customers against the more dangerous cars and thus reduce bloodshed.

All that's required is one honest insurance-company chief executive:

1. His computer tells him that a particular automobile is involved in an exceptionally large percentage of accidents.
2. He discloses this to a few important customers.
3. He gets sued for giving information to some customers and not to others.
4. He loses the case in such a way that, henceforth, all insurance companies must supply data to the public on exceptionally dangerous vehicles.

This is only one example.

Hey, you out there! Think of the most important area where your industry would be serving the public interest if it had one honest chief-executive officer.

Does it alarm you to know that your industry doesn't have a single honest chief executive?

Me, too.

CUTBACK. When the squeeze is on, call in all the people who report to you—in one room, if possible, so they'll all get the same message.

Tell them, "Don't answer this now. Come in tomorrow with the answer in pencil on a piece of paper, so the secretaries don't start a panic":

If you had to eliminate some activities under your control (not just cut them back), in which order would you eliminate them?

I want a ten per cent reduction in expenses from everybody. No hanky-panky. Don't eliminate an activity by transferring it to a different department.

This is painful, but it *can* be turned to an advantage. You probably have some vital activities that are understaffed. If you can chop fifteen per cent instead of ten per cent, you can have the extra five per cent to feed your starving tigers.

Use this emergency to pull up *all* your weeds. If it's done now, the organization won't go into shock. Give me a legitimate ten per cent expense reduction and plow the rest back wherever you think it should go, or save it until you *know* where it should go.

I know this sounds like the old Hoosier saw, "When they hand you a lemon—make lemonade," but the capacity of people to find answers, if they know it's worth the trouble, has never been tested to its practical limits.

Before you call your people in, make sure you've got the answer for your own office—and tell them what it is—even if it's just a ten per cent cut in your own salary. You can't expect to be taken seriously if you're sitting there with three secretaries and two assistants playing grab-ass outside your office. Don't pull an L.B.J. at the light switch, either—unless you, too, want to be a joke.

GROWTH FEVER. Almost everybody subscribes to the myth that a company has to keep growing. "If you stand still, you die," they say.

I don't know which idiot first carved this imperative on the tablet.

If your company comes to a plateau in earnings, take the time to look around and get your bearings. You may discover a whole new direction.

You don't necessarily have to spend your life trying to extend last year's graphs.

The typical corporate reaction to a leveling off in earnings comes perilously close to the knee jerk that philosopher George Santayana warned about: "Fanaticism consists in redoubling your efforts when you have forgotten your aim."

ACQUISITIONS I: How to pick 'em. The best acquisitions will look overpriced and you'll be tempted to veto them on that score. Don't—not if everything else looks right.

The bag of snakes will come disguised as an ever-loving blue-eyed bargain.

ACQUISITIONS II: Lock up the lawyers. Memorandums of intent are devilish devices that boost legal fees and cut the chances of a deal's going through.

When two companies have reached an agreement, the two principals and their lawyers, accountants and other necessary associates should meet and start drawing up the final contract—not a memorandum of intent to agree.

I don't know how much time and effort I wasted before discovering that deals aren't usually blown by principals; they're blown by lawyers and accountants trying to prove how valuable they are.

If nobody gets to go home for dinner or if the possibility arises of having to cancel that Saturday-morning golf game, you'll be surprised how quickly problems are solved.

If the two groups split up for the weekend, their lawyers will have dreamed up enough bright ideas by Monday morning to take them miles apart—even though the deal was actually in the bag on Friday night.

If everyone stays in the same room, each smart-ass idea will be rejected or negotiated while the contract is being written.

This concept is even more important in the present era of instant disclosure. When you walk out of a locked-door closing, you announce that a deal was done. Let your lazy lawyers talk you into a memorandum of intent and all you announce to the world is that if anybody wants to queer this agreement, he'd better get moving.

Don't forget the corporate seals, round-the-clock typists and a notary public. You can't go home until that document is signed, witnessed and notarized.

BREVITY. The usual way to sell an idea to a board of directors is to produce a stack of bulky reports in brown, red, black or gray leatherette binders and hand them out to anyone who might be concerned. Days later, when the subject comes up for discussion, one third of those present won't have read the report, one third will have read enough to induce merciful black-out and the remaining third, those opposed to the project, will have read carefully and assembled enough arguments to kill it outright or delay it indefinitely.

The next time you have to make a pitch in a board room, try it without notes, charts, handouts or assistants. Remember:

1. Most people with power would like to use it wisely, if someone believable would tell them how.
2. They know that any proposal having to do with their business can be stated clearly and completely in less than one minute.

Why not help them out? When you know your subject cold and have a conviction, make the pitch orally. Stay under a minute. Avoid all props and end with a request for action.

NO-NO'S; PISSING IN THE SOUP.

- Pension plans for top people. Security is for people who don't have a chance to make it big. Above a certain level (you pick it), don't have pensions. Encourage your people to build their own security by building the company they own a piece of.
- Taking phone calls in meetings: "Look at me, I'm busy!" If you get a phone call from Nixon, how much more impressive to *not* take it. Besides, your refusal will strike panic into those 19 Medusas on the White House switchboard, who believe they have the divine right to interrupt anybody, anywhere, any time.
- Tax dodges. Encouraging your people—with company cars and company apartments—to take their eyes off profit building and focus on tax-saving schemes instead.

- Synergism, a business fad like hula hoops, holds that two and two makes five. Horseshit. Two and two usually makes three, and you know it. Because divisions forced to deal with one another learn to hate with a passion—and find ways to take it out on one another.

- Consistency is something you have to be inconsistent about. With a nationwide franchise agreement, be consistent; if you permit one variation, the finger is out of the dike. But where the advantages far outweigh the disadvantages—such as letting people set their own office hours and firing those who consistently abuse that freedom—you must be consistently inconsistent.

- Jet set. There may come a time when your corporate fame is such that the beautiful people honor you with offers of their services. Decline.

- Liquor and drugs. Don't try to tell people how to conduct themselves at home. But if someone comes to the office zonked a third time, fire him without bothering to find out what he's using.

DO IT NOW. The telephone is still underused. How many times have you read something and said to yourself: "I need to *talk* to him"? You may never meet him, but chances are you *can* talk to him. Pick up the phone. Now.

You'll discover that, in this respect, the world is divided into self-important asses and authentic humans. You won't be able to get through to the former, and that's a pretty good indication they're not worth talking to. The others will be surprisingly easy to reach—and happy you called. Who isn't pleased to learn that somebody out there cares?

But call him now. While the urge is on you. Otherwise, you'll just be adding to that giant trash can of good ideas you once had but never acted on.

POLAROID POWER. If you're responsible for a group of hamburger stands, service stations, banks, nursing homes or supermarkets, where appearance is critical, take a Polaroid camera along on your trips. If you see an obsolete sign, a dirty counter or a slovenly employee, take a picture. Show it to the manager. Tell him it will be prominently featured in your rogues' gallery back home until he sends you a picture of the new look.

Worth a thousand words? More like a million.

MERCY MISPLACED. The average leader avoids prescribing corporate euthanasia for a limping company operation. Why? Not because he can't read the numbers—he's sharp enough with those. Because he came up through a system that excessively rewards the ability to get along with other people.

Mercy may help him get along for the moment. But misplaced mercy is seldom merciful. As a result of his soft-headed decision, bright, able people get trapped in an obsolete division. They bust their humps fighting to salvage a lost cause.

The standard performance-appraisal sheet offers a constant reminder of how far off the track we are with respect to the qualities we need in our leaders. It emphasizes the self-serving skills of the corporate politicians who can't come up with hard decisions that are *truly* merciful in the long run.

"Flexibility," "Adaptability," "Gets along well with others." I don't believe they're what's needed today if we're going to force our institutions to adapt to *us*—which is our central problem.

The Ottoman Turks for over three centuries produced an unbroken succession of able leaders. Their performance-appraisal sheet would have looked like this:

Adaptability	0
Adventuresomeness	100
Cruelty	100
Energy	100
Flexibility	0
Intelligence	100
Justice	100
Gets along well with others	0

Please note—Justice, 100. Without that, they would have been nothing.

May I suggest that if you don't start developing your own Ottoman Turks, pretty soon they'll be coming over the walls?

SWING LOW, SWEET SUPPLICANT.

1. John Bigdeal, senior vice-president, when he needs an important approval from a regulatory agency, calls someone at or near the top, takes him to lunch, explains in detail and hands him his written application with a friendly request for expedition. The application goes down to Bill Overworked, dedicated staffer, who is enraged at having something jammed into his part of the pipeline. He takes one of two courses: (A) buries it; or (B) works all night building an airtight case against approval, or at least asking enough tough questions so that when the answers come back, he'll be able to ask twice as many more.

2. Fred Humble, senior vice-president, finds the appropriate *bottom* level in the regulatory-agency staff, takes Bill Overworked to lunch and gives him the application. Since Bill has never met a senior vice-president before, that application tends to get his top priority. Humble can now needle it gracefully up the pipeline by calling Bill Overworked

and asking whose desk it's on now and then taking *him* to lunch.

Who do you think gets the approval first?

This applies to working with all bureaucracies, inside and outside your company. I just picked regulatory agencies as an example.

A HEALTHY FEAR OF SUCCESS. People tend to learn from failure. When success arrives, however, they don't ask why and they don't try to learn from it. They go home and tell their wives how smart they are.

Take an unaccountable, unexplained and excessive run-up in the price of your stock.

For years, you've been wooing security analysts. Then one day, they all discover your stock. In a month, it runs up from 20 to 50 times earnings.

That's success! The ultimate pay-off! Wow!

What you should do, of course, instead of congratulating yourself, is call a press conference and tell the world you think the run-up is silly, that you don't know of anything to justify it and that you personally plan to sell some of your stock, if the price holds.

Instead, however, you'll probably accept the telephone congratulations of your directors, and then, in a panic, you'll look around for something—anything—that might justify the new price of the stock.

That new merger you didn't like now looks good.

That half-baked new product line might be the answer. Maybe that big computerization program will cut costs.

Goodbye, baby.

Your successor will pick up the pieces. And all because you didn't have the guts to say you thought your own stock was overpriced.

CORPORATE IMAGE. Among the many serious blows American business has suffered, none was more devastating than that delivered by the public-relations man who first applied the word image to a corporation and its executives. The result has been a massive misapplication of national energy and assets roughly rivaling the cost of a moon shot. Grown men who should be engaged in more serious activities have been spending millions of dollars and whole careers on silly speeches, institutional advertising and annual reports that look like a Sunday supplement.

Repent, for the Day of Judgment is never far away. Whatever appeal may be created by a corporate-image campaign will fade fast and sure. The only image you should care about is the smile on the face of your customer as he enjoys your product or service, or on the face of your stockholder as he scans the company profits.

VANITY, ALL IS VANITY: The annual report. Take away the words and numbers required by the SEC, N.Y.S.E. and the C.P.A. firm as the price of their clean certificate. What's left? A picture of chairman J. B. Bloat and president B. Lemuel Phat, faces twisted into unwonted grins, congratulating each other on having gotten away with it for another year.

Next come a few expensive pictures of "operations" with black employees on the job—both of them hauled out of the basement, dressed up in clean uniforms and placed prominently in the left foreground. The numbers and pictures float around a badly written, one-sided puff piece.

If all the U.S. dollars wasted in the past five years on this corporate flatulence had been devoted to rebuilding the ghettos, white businessmen would be lunching in Harlem and taking the wife and kids to Watts for vacations.

But, as William F. Buckley, Jr., must have said, altruism is not the corporate bag.

So here is a viable alternative: Let corporations give really creative support to the graphic arts. Suppose the Z Corporation, at the beginning of its fiscal year, hired a good struggling writer, a good struggling artist and a good struggling photographer and said to them, "We want a 25,000-word report to the stockholders, employees and customers of our company that will give them the absolute truth about us—the good, bad, sad and funny—and the real heroes and villains of the year just beginning. And if we catch you accepting threats or bribes from anyone, you will be summarily dismissed."

Think of it! The picture in front would show the tired but happy bunch of physicists who unlocked the secret of one-coat, quick-drying lifetime paint. And a little box on the page would note the early retirement of vice-president Harry ("Iron Duke") Kelly, who tried to bury the discovery because it would put the company paint division and all of its competitors out of business in three years.

Anybody got the guts to try it? If so, I urge you to make it a three-year project, with a different team each year.

And don't choke if you have a bad year. Your annual report may well be the best thing you produce.

ACKNOWLEDGMENTS

Having no secretary and an unreadable hand, I was doubly blessed with the unfailing help of Starr Johnson (Moonlight West) and Angie Abbatello (Moonlight East). Thank you.

David Dushkin steered me to Bob Gottlieb and Tony Schulte at Knopf, for which I'm grateful: when you have to deal with a stark raving mad industry like book publishing, it's well to deal directly with the head lunatics. Emmet Hughes and Lew Estrin gave valuable thinking and criticism, for which I thank them.

T George Harris gave invaluable encouragement and help before and during the writing. It's perfectly safe to say that if he hadn't been around to push, the book wouldn't have been written.

It would be unthinkable not to mention the educational value of my fourteen years at American Express. During those years (1948–62) the company was rich enough to do—and did—almost everything wrong. In that near-perfect learning environment I formed the valuable habit of observing what action was taken, considering the *opposite* course, and then working back, when necessary, to what really made sense.

For the past ten years, Donald Petrie and Jerry Hardy, two voices laughing hysterically in the institutional wilderness, have kept telling me that just because we were alone didn't mean that we were wrong. Without their ideas and reinforcement, I'd have probably given up before the conclusive (to us) opportunity to test this pattern of management came along.

Appendix A:
Townsend's Third
Degree in Leadership

Editor's Note: The following is the edited text of an address to the Conference Board, which was printed as an article in Across the Board *in the late 1970s. Reprinted with permission.*

I'm going to try to give all of you a Ph.D. in leadership.

The **first lesson** is: *To hell with centralized strategic planning.* If you don't have a good leader, it's all nothing; it's just a bunch of papers flying around.

Let me tell you what leadership is not. In some companies the chief executive has retired on the payroll, and there aren't any leaders. The companies are run by strong planning departments, strong purchasing departments, strong human-resources departments, and strong management-information services. What generally happens in those strong staff organizations is that you get very mediocre performance from otherwise able people down the line.

Some companies have gotten out of that trap. I'll give you one: Kollmorgen, 5,000 people, 16 divisions, had a marvelous management information system with a 360 computer to tell everybody in the company wherever a sparrow fell. The whole company was so mesmerized with information that nobody did anything. And, bless his heart, Bob Swiggett the CEO, practically over the dead body of the Harvard Business

School, which was telling him to centralize management-information services, shot the 360 computer between the eyes. He called up his 16 division presidents and said, "I am instituting a return-on-net-assets incentive compensation system for all of you; I want you to think of your divisions as if you owned them, and telephone in 10 numbers every month so that I can consolidate a P & L and a balance sheet."

Well, the organization came to life. It became a much more profitable, good, fun place to work. It turned around fast, without any consultants. They didn't have a strategic planning department to think about it for three years; they just did it.

The **second point** about leadership I learned while working for American Express many years ago. I was a security analyst, and I worked for a boss who was very typical of bosses then and maybe now.

He was tall; he was handsome; he was ambitious, intelligent, articulate; and he was never there when we needed him. *He took credit for everything we did that was any good and blamed us for everything that went wrong.* We spent all our time coming in late and leaving early and bitching about the conditions. We were all underpaid; we didn't have the right mix of people.

All of a sudden he died, and the company in its infinite wisdom named me head of the investment department. I called everybody in and said, "I don't know anything about management; I'm very uncomfortable. But one thing's for sure: We don't have to talk about what's wrong; we haven't been doing anything else since I've been here. Why don't you people form a partnership and be the best investment department you can," I said, "and I'll try to get us the proper pay, the proper titles, the proper machinery, and the proper mix of people." And they said, "That's a pretty good idea, because you're a lousy analyst anyway, and we won't miss you."

So I did. I started to go around. And these people started coming in early and doing good work and making good decisions. And I remember one: Bobby Clarkson, who was chairman of the board, stopped me in the hall and said, "Townsend, that was a good bond swap you made last week." And I said, "Bond swap? I don't know anything about a bond swap. I don't even get to read the *Wall Street Journal*." I said, "I'm working full time to get bowls of rice for my peons, so they don't starve on your front steps and embarrass you."

Well gradually we started getting what we should be paid, and the titles we should have, so we could go in and interview top management. And I got more and more power from their performance, and one day Charlie Cuccinello, who invested our traveller's check float, which was billions of dollars in short-term securities, came to me, "If I had one of the new Japanese calculators," he said, "instead of the hand-crank machines I have been using" (his predecessor used an abacus—this was an old company), "I could make us a ton of money." I said, "Charlie, you're right, you're absolutely right. Why didn't I think of that? I'll go get you one."

Listen, that's what a leader does. He doesn't say, "I'll call in one of my three secretaries and dictate a purchase requisition, which will sit in some out-box for three days, and when it gets back to me for my signature I'll be in Europe, so it will wait until I get back and will just miss the three-monthly purchasing meeting, and it will be two months later when it is returned to me rejected." I said, "I'll go get you one."

So I get in the elevator and go down to the fifth floor to the purchasing department, and say, "Hi, my name's Townsend. I work up on the fourteenth floor and I need an electronic calculator, and here's the make and model number."

And the man on duty says, "Is it in your budget?" And I say, "No, it isn't, because I made my budget out last October, and I only found out I needed it today. So I've come to my purchasing department for help." The purchasing man says, "If it's not in your budget, you can't have it."

I was carrying my resignation around, so I pulled it out—it was battered. I said, "Would you please sign this," and he looked at it and he read it and said, "Why should I sign that? That's your resignation, and you don't work for me." I said, "Because when I leave here I'm going up to the president's office, to whom I report, and I'm going to resign. He may ask me why I'm resigning, and if he does, I'm going to tell him it's because some stupid son of a bitch in the purchasing department won't give me a machine that would pay for itself the first two and a half minutes that we owned it. And if he asks me which stupid son of a bitch in the purchasing department, I want to show him your name."

Well, we got the machine. But that's not the point. The real point is that I was using the power that those people in the investment department were giving me not to get goodies for myself, but to get things for them, to enable them to do the job even better. If you ever break that circle and start stealing the goodies that come from their performance, they'll find out about it, and they'll stop cooking and they'll stop trying, and you won't know what turned the organization off.

What I was really doing, though I didn't know it at the time, and this is the lesson for your Leadership Kit: *was eliminating their excuses for doing lousy work.* An excuse may be just "I'm underpaid," or "I'm undertitled," or "We really don't have the right kind of people here," or "We don't have an economist." I was eliminating their excuses.

At Avis I discovered another principle of leadership, which is to *fight the them-and-us lines that separate people in a company.* These lines are easy to see. There are the people you trust and the people you don't trust. The people you don't trust park outside the gate, have to punch the time clock, and have to get coffee out of a coffee machine. The people you trust park inside, don't punch the time clock, and get free coffee. You want to fight those lines.

One of the interesting lines in America is that the difference in salary between the CEO and the highest paid blue-collar worker is 36 to 1; in Japan it's 7 to 1. Now that's a them-us line that I think hard to swallow, knowing what chief executives don't do for their companies.

The way we got around it at Avis was that we had one rental agent school taught by our finest rental agents, ladies in red uniforms. It was a tough school, at O'Hare Airport, with an exam every night. I made the whole management go through it; it is an absolute condition of employment. We had to study, and we had to spend two or three hours renting cars at the airport.

I went through it, too. One night, I had my trainee button on and was renting a car and was trying to get the right keys with the right agreement—this was before the computer did this. I was trying to get the figures in the right boxes. When my customer said, "Can't you hurry up? I'm on a real bummer of a trip." I said. "Give me a break, I'm a trainee." I kept on doing it, and I dropped the keys, and he said, "You're certainly the worst trainee I ever saw. Where did they dig you up from?" And I said, "You want to know something really sick? I'm the president of the company."

I tell you when we got back to headquarters we were so proud of those ladies out there on the firing line and the difficulty of the job that they were doing that we started wearing red jackets around the executive office as a sign that we were part of their team. When we went into a city, we'd look at them with different eyes; they were our heroines now, instead of being the dopes who were renting cars.

As you know *I have recommended that you fire all your management consultants,* all of them. Promise them a bonus if they will get off the premises by 5 P.M. and another bonus if they won't submit a report. Let me explain this to you.

Let's say we've got three divisions in a mythical company and you are the chief executive. You have already gone to four board meetings a year, so you're already in that mode. You have three divisions. It's old Joe's division. He keeps reorganizing, missing his target, reorganizing, missing his targets. It's time to face up to the fact that the old log is no longer the guy to run that division. So you say to your board, "I'm going to go over and run old Joe's division for three months, and I'll see what's going on." You tell old Joe to go skiing in Vail or go to Palm Springs and play golf with Gerry Ford or something. You say that when he comes back there will be a job with equal pay and benefits, but it sure as hell will not be running this division.

And then—and this is very important—*you actually go over and sit at Joe's desk.* You don't bring anybody with you, like your secretary, to make your life comfortable; you go sit at old Joe's desk. You call everybody in who reported to old Joe, and you say, "Now you people know a lot about this problem. I'm your new division president, by the way. You all know a lot about and you all have different views about what it will take to make this thing cook. I'm going to call you in one at a time and ask you for your help. But I don't want your goddamn private grievances committee; I don't want to hear about any goddamn coffeepots. I want you to tell me how to save this division and make it a credit to the company, because if we can't do this in a relatively short period of time, I'm going to shut the mother down."

Now that's motivation.

Contrast that with the normal approach of the big company, in which the chief executive is too lazy to get out of his office and give up all those comfortable surroundings. He calls McKinsey & Company and drops six Harvard Business School graduates on these poor beleaguered people. Then they *know* they are in trouble. They might love to solve the problem themselves. But now you have to educate six people who don't know anything about the business.

Now, let us go back to the alternative. You are sitting in old Joe's chair and you may have to call in your people one at a time, three times each, but at some point you'll wake up and they will have given you the plan of how to turn that thing around. Then you call everybody in and say, "This is the plan you have given me, this is what you want to do, and Bill, you are the obvious one to run the division and carry out this plan; if you want to change it tomorrow because you run into something, change it. I just want you to save this division and make it a credit.

In six months those people will be 10 feet tall, and they will have forgotten that you were ever there. And it's all very proper that they do so, because they really did save the division themselves, and you'll be back in your own office with your cockamamie outside directors.

For the final part of your Ph.D., I'm going to tell you from my experience *the characteristics of a leader.*

This is something that's very important and very difficult and misunderstood. They come in all shapes and sizes and colors and sexes; some are bright, some are dull, some are articulate, some can't speak a whole sentence, some are Type A's, some are lazy and laid-back. You cannot recognize them physically. Charisma is not generally associated with a true leader, in my opinion. It is more associated with the opposite: the *corporate politician,* who is what is the matter with our country. There are too many of this type in our corner offices.

Leaders have their *personal ambition under control;* they seem to get their kicks out of seeing their own people succeed and their own organization succeed. *They are visible or available* to their people, and they are *good listeners*. Listening is a very painful thing because, depending on how much pain they're in, you may have to listen to your people say something four or five times until they get that look in their eyes that says, "By golly, he really understands." When they get that look, you can say, "Fred, I understand what you're saying. Now get the hell back to work and do it my way."

Then they'll go back home, and they cry like babies and tell their spouses, "At least the son of a bitch listened."

That takes the anger out, but it's very painful to the listener. That's why you need a new CEO every five or six years, because after five or six years he or she can't listen anymore.

A good leader is decisive. This is why you should not have lawyers or accountants or MBAs in a corner office. They want to get the last shred and scrap of information; they are happy with numbers and words, and they don't trust people. They need more information, and by the time they have collected all the information for the decision, the timing is off and they might as well forget the whole project.

At some point a good leader with inadequate data will say, "Ready, fire, aim . . . and if it doesn't work we'll correct it, but at least the timing is right to start with what we have."

A good leader *sees the best in his people,* not the worst; he is not a scapegoat hunter. He sees winners, and he uses "the rule of 50 percent," which makes him high on promoting from within. The rule is that if you have anybody in your organization who looks like 50 percent of what you need for a job and who has the support of the people around her and wants the job, give this person the job and she'll grow the other 50 percent.

The corporate politician with no faith in his people hires a search firm, and they wind up bringing in an electric blue suit. He raises salaries all around, and a year later you're still teaching him the business. A good leader is simplistic, not complex. He makes *things seem simple. He's persistent.* If he can't convince his people and he really thinks it ought to be done, he'll find a different way to come at them until either they convince him, or he them.

He's *fair and has a sense of humor,* and he has *humility.* If you ever become chief executive, remember: You are still the same lovable, stupid lazy slob you were the day before you got the job, and don't try to rush out and buy a whole lot of three-piece suits to fool people. You're not going to fool anybody. You got there on your program, so *stay on your program.* But just remember to work a lot harder, and work for your people.

About the time of my first meeting with the board at Avis, General Sarnoff did what all outside directors do: They try to impress the other outside directors with how smart they are. He said, "I would like a run of all the cars we have in Avis, by the location and model number." I thought of the weeks that that would take our accounting department to run down, and I said to him, "General, if I don't need that statement to run the company, you sure as hell don't need it to be an outside director of the company."

Bless his heart, the general turned purple; it was a joy for me to behold it.

But what I was doing was protecting my people, so they could get on with what the company was really trying to do. It was also in the first 100 days; the man who hired you can't fire you without looking stupid.

I suppose the best way to tell a leader is, if you find a place where people are coming to work enthusiastically and they are excited to come to work and would rather work there than anywhere else, you can bet you have got a leader.

Well, there's your Ph.D. in leadership.

Good luck and God bless.

Appendix B:
No Reserved Parking:
The Guerrilla Life of
Robert Townsend

Robert Townsend Jr.

Robert Chase Townsend was born in Washington, D.C., on July 30, 1920, the younger son of Clinton Paul Townsend, a chemist and patent attorney, and his second wife, Katherine Moses Townsend. He had one sibling, a half-brother, Blake.

The Townsends moved to Great Neck, New York, in the early 1920s; young Robert later boarded at the Lawrenceville School and attended Princeton University, where he majored in English literature. Although his early life was marked by upper-middle-class privilege, it was not without challenge and sadness: his father died unexpectedly after an accident when Townsend was thirteen years old. Robert would always evince some ambivalence about growing up in advantaged surroundings; he exhibited an egalitarian streak and resented any displays of ostentation, nepotism, or elitism. He was quoted as saying, "Too much inherited money is a birth defect."

Robert met his future wife (and love of his life), Joan Tours, in Great Neck during a visit home from school; they were to maintain a steady correspondence throughout his years at Princeton and after he enlisted in the Navy in 1941 following Pearl Harbor. Robert and Joan were married while he was on shore leave in San Diego in 1944. Their first child, Katherine Joan, was born while Robert was still at sea.

At the conclusion of the war, "Towny" and Joan returned to New York. Townsend's first position in business was as a securities analyst for Haas Securities on Wall Street; the firm encouraged him to pursue a degree in business, and he enrolled at Columbia University's business school, taking classes at night. Now the proud parents of two young daughters (Joan Patrice was born in April 1946), the young Townsend family moved from Manhattan to Long Island, and Townsend commuted into the city every day for the next decade or so. Three more children followed: Robert Chase Jr., Claire Tracy, and Jeffrey Tours.

In 1950, Townsend joined the American Express Company, where, by his own account, he spent nearly fifteen years learning how *not* to manage a business. While at Amex, Townsend undertook what he later termed "Operation Mars," a joint venture between American Express and Hertz Rent-a-Car. He called it Operation Mars because he understood that this project (to reorganize Hertz as a worldwide car rental agency) would require long absences over a period of two years or more, and that he "might as well be on a trip to Mars." It was this project that formed the basis for his enduring friendship and partnership with Donald Petrie, his counterpart at Hertz. Townsend later dedicated his book *Up the Organization* to Petrie.

After the successful completion of Operation Mars, Petrie was approached by the partnership that had taken control of the ailing Avis Rent-a-Car Company. Avis's board was looking for a new CEO, and offered the position to Petrie, who declined. He did, however, recommend Townsend for the job, which Townsend held from 1962 to 1965. Petrie did join Avis and Townsend as a senior executive and helped him move the company's headquarters from Boston, Massachusetts, to Garden City, New York. Under Townsend's iconoclastic leadership, and boosted by a successful ad campaign—"We Try Harder"—Avis was transformed into a worldwide, world-class organization.

Avis's increasing fortunes attracted takeover artist Harold Geneen and his wildly acquisitive ITT, which acquired Avis in 1965. Townsend strongly disapproved of conglomerates in general and ITT in particular, and soon resigned from the newly merged company. He makes oblique reference to his resignation in this book: "If you have a good company, don't sell out to a conglomerate; I was sold out once and resigned (*see* Disobedience and Its Necessity)."

Liberated from his corporate ties, Townsend was free to pursue his self-appointed mission to transform ailing corporations into fun and profitable enterprises. It was during one of these "missions," with CRM, Inc., of Del Mar, California, that Townsend discovered his mixed feelings about being a consultant. (He originated the phrase "Consultants are the people who borrow your watch to tell you what time it is and then walk off with it.") As a notice of resignation, he composed a long typewritten "memo"—"The ABC Survival Manual"—and ran off copies on the company's mimeograph machine. When they arrived the next morning, each CRM employee found one stapled copy on his or her chair or desk.

His CRM clients encouraged Townsend to expand the memo into a book, and a writing career was born. Townsend returned to Locust Valley, New York, rented a small office over the town barbershop, and, with Knopf editor Robert Gottlieb, honed his survival guide into the book that you're holding in your hands. As Gottlieb reports in his account, the publication of *Up the Organization* became a massive sensation and propelled Townsend to celebrity status; he appeared on the *Tonight Show,* was profiled in *Playboy,* and was lauded by iconoclasts as diverse as Ralph Nader and Betty Friedan.

In the years that followed, Townsend pursued an uneasy flirtation with retirement; he was never particularly good at it. In 1974, he and Joan moved to Los Angeles to see if "retirement" might be easier in Southern California. It wasn't.

His now-grown children were more or less scattered over the world, but his youngest daughter, Claire, was living in Los Angeles and experiencing some success as an executive at 20th Century Fox. With the phenomenal success of its *Star Wars* in 1977, Fox found itself on the horns of a dilemma. When the studio began raking in money, Alan Ladd, Jr. and his California team discovered that the New York "suits and bean counters" now felt required to insert themselves into the creative process to a far greater extent.

In 1978, during a weekly "story meeting" at the studio in Century City, "Laddie" and the crew were discussing the problem, at which point Claire piped up with the suggestion that they hire her dad; he would be the perfect person to run interference with the bean counters while the creative types could get on with the business of making movies. "And besides," she added, "he's driving my mother nuts, hanging around the house all day."

Ironically (given Townsend's frequent railings against nepotism), Fox's corporate charter included an antinepotism provision, and a meeting of the board had to be convened to waive the rule so that they could hire Townsend. For the next few years, Townsend was in his element once again—working on the "inside," influencing corporate policy, making working for a corporation fun and profitable. During that time Townsend also dipped his toe into a small number of other business ventures, as an investor, adviser, or board member. These included Leadership Directories, Inc.; Dun & Bradstreet; IGT; and Radica Games, now a subsidiary of Mattel. (See essay by Bob Davids.)

Although he was essentially banned from NBC after his *Tonight Show* appearance criticizing NBC management, Robert remained in public life. In 1984, he published *Further Up the Organization,* including additional material and revising some of the language that he had come to feel was sexist and insufficiently sensitive to the emerging female executive class. This new edition remained on the *New York Times* list for a respectable nine weeks. Later in the decade, he released two updated audio versions of the book. He was extremely popular as a speaker (his speech to the Conference Board is included in this new edition), and later taped discussions with Tom Peters *(Excellence in the Organization),* in whom he found a kindred spirit. In 1994, he published a quirky book about the generation gap, *The B2 Chronicles.* Townsend maintained a long friendship with Warren Bennis, which began when Townsend "cold-called" Bennis during his MIT years. Townsend's last writing project was a collaborative effort with Bennis: *Reinventing Leadership: Strategies to Empower the Organization* (Morrow, 1995).

In 1991, Townsend was diagnosed with heart disease and underwent emergency triple bypass surgery. He made a difficult recovery and seemed to soften a bit in his stridency as a corporate critic. He continued to enjoy sailing off the California coast and perfecting his golf game. In 1998, he and Joan chartered a ketch in the Caribbean and planned a lengthy vacation. On a clear, moonlit night in Anguilla's harbor, he took a chair on deck and began to trade fishing stories with the sailboat captain. After what seemed like a typical thoughtful pause, he lay his chin down and slipped away.

The *New York Times* interviewed Ralph Nader for its lengthy obituary of Townsend: "Robert Townsend was a witty and incisive archenemy of corporate bureaucracy. A creative business iconoclast and human relations genius, he succeeded in business by challenging and replacing the ossified conventions of corporate management. *Up the Organization* is a classic in putting people first in business."